THE MODERN
SEER

Jim Driscoll's book, *The Modern Seer,* is very practical and a much needed guide to help people develop and understand the seer-prophetic gifting. He reveals God's hidden language of metaphor and symbolism in deep yet simple ways. The practical exercises make this a true handbook that you will refer to again and again.

Doug Addison
Author of *Prophecy, Dreams, and Evangelism*
www.dougaddison.com

Jim Driscoll's book, *The Modern Seer*, is an excellent resource in this season for both spiritual leadership and those called to be seers. Jim shares incredible insight to the function and maturation process of the seer. This book strengthens one's understanding of the realm of the spirit and will help hone your interpretive skills. Jim's experience, wisdom, and understanding have been personally valuable to me. For those who desire deeper knowledge of the things of the Spirit, you need to read this book!

Aaron Evans
The Emerging Daniel Company International
www.emergingdanielcompany.org

In *The Modern Seer*, Jim has captured what few before him have: the experience and understanding of not only how to operate in the seer gift, but how to use it in a safe and constructive way. This book can help all of the Church understand how to operate in the gifts of spiritual sensitivity.

Zach Mapes
European Director, Stir The Water
www.stirthewater.com/zach

I am excited that *The Modern Seer* is soon to be in print. There has been a plethora of books written over the last twenty years regarding the revelatory gifts of the Holy Spirit for today. Jim's book stands out for several excellent reasons. First, it is Biblically based. So much of what has recently been written is highly subjective with little Bible to help the average person understand true foundations for having spiritual "eyes to see and ears to hear." Secondly, I applaud Jim's focus on the priesthood of every believer. It is everyone's birthright, who belongs to Christ Jesus, to be led by the Spirit. Jim has done an excellent job at both de-mystifying revelation and putting it in hands of everyday Christians. Thirdly, this book does not consist of merely rehashing popular insights regarding revelation. Many of Driscoll's points are both fresh and extremely helpful. For example, chapter 9, which discusses how deeply God values kindness and the Biblical relationship of kindness with seeing and applying revelation will prove to be of immense help to many who are both starting out in revelation and those who are experienced in it. Thank you, Jim, for writing this! It will encourage, train, and safeguard many, many people in the years ahead.

MARC A. DUPONT
MANTLE OF PRAISE MINISTRIES, INC.
WWW.MARCDUPONTMINISTRIES.ORG

Jim Driscoll delivers a book that will shift and change our spiritual realities. Never has anyone so clearly described what it means to be a seer. Jim delivers his message in clear and concise terms, understandable to both the spiritual expert and novice alike. Provided within are highly recommended tools necessary to unlock and move forward in the seer gifting.

SCOTT ALLEN
CEO, IFORMATA COMMUNICATIONS

Herein is wisdom and rich encouragement. These are the words of a man who has studied and practiced his gifting — who has persevered through blunders, misunderstanding, and pain. Presented with characteristic humility and simplicity of style, The Modern Seer comes from years of seeking to enable others. It is the product of a heart with a love of Christ and a compassion for people.

Don't just read this book and set it aside. Live with it. Open your Bible, seek God, and practice the exercises. Then read it again, another time. There is maturity in its pages and there is much to learn from Jim's insights. Let God expand your horizons. Grow in faith and understanding. Let the eyes of your heart awaken to the unseen.

Rev. David J Torrance
Minister in the Church of Scotland, UK

I have known Jim Driscoll for a good number of years. I have ministered alongside of him in conferences, and he has also ministered numerous time in the church in which I am a leader. I have personally watched the Lord touch, inspire, equip, and encourage many people through the prophetic ministry that flows through Jim. I believe this book is and will be a great extension of that prophetic ministry. As a pastor and overseer of churches, I am excited for the people of our churches to have a resource such as this book to equip and inspire them in their giftings. I believe that whoever reads and applies the truths that Jim has written in this book will go to new levels of their relationship to the Lord and experience greater clarity in his/her giftings.

Richard Sizemore
Founder of:
Dwelling Place Christian Fellowship
and
Dwelling Place International Ministries

THE MODERN
SEER

A Biblical Gift in Today's Context

Jim Driscoll

The Modern Seer: A Biblical Gift in Today's Context
© Copyright 2010 Jim Driscoll

orbital
BOOK GROUP

Published by Orbital Book Group
www.orbitalbookgroup.com

Cover art by Trace Chiodo
Interior design by Bethany Leone

ISBN: 978-0-9822821-0-6
LCCN: 2009934449

Printed in the United States of America.

For information on this title and others:
Visit www.orbitalbookgroup.com

To pastors and leaders everywhere
who show patience, grace, and value
for emerging, maturing seers.

Contents

THE MODERN
SEER

INTRODUCTION
By Gregory Mapes

I have known Bob Jones and called him my friend for about twenty-five years. During that time, we have been close and we have been distant, and I have seen him soar with the eagles and scrape the bottom of the barrel. Whether he was at the top or at the bottom, he was always full of God's love and never stopped knowing stuff. I know of nobody I'd rather have pray for me or my family members' deliverance from spiritual oppression, mess, or for healing.

When Bob has told me deep spiritual things over the years, I have usually needed him to go over them several times to actually understand what he told me. Primarily that is because our culture has weeded out the specialized language of the seer as we have become largely a non-sensing people in the West. *The Modern Seer* by Jim Driscoll is an effort to establish not only a description of the seer but to help build a vocabulary that encourages seers to come into communication with one another and others who may not have the seer gift.

Part of interacting with seers is the wonderful experience of being there smelling, tasting, hearing, seeing, and touching right along with them. I have been friends with Jim going on ten years. Jim is just as "strange" as Bob when it comes to spiritual experiences and knowings. Both Jim and Bob are very intelligent and do well handling the Word of God. The one thing that impresses me most about Jim's ministry, and Bob's, too, is that they have in common the ability to love the Person Jesus and allow themselves to be used for the glory of God no matter how foolish or absurd they appear to the observers around them. They both love the Body of Christ and desire the best for the Church even at their own expense. There is a genuine kindness not often found in men of national reputation. If he stays the course, I expect that in the coming years Jim will rise to the same kind of prominence that Bob has had. I've seen the fruit of their ministries and their lives, and it tastes good.

FOREWORD
By Bob Jones

What is a seer? A seer is everything. Prophets are the eyes, but seers are the entire head: eyes, ears, smell, taste, and feelings. That is what Isaiah 29:10 says:

He has shut your eyes, the prophets;
And He has covered your heads, the seers.

A seer is everything. I like to use a hot loaf of bread to explain this gifting. With your eyes open, you can see it. But if your eyes are closed, I can tell you it is there, and you will be able to "see" it with your ears. I can put it under your nose, and you can smell it. I can put it in your mouth, and you can taste it. You can feel it in your hands. As a seer, you move in all five realms, and because of that, you are more discerning. The enemy is never able to fully shut you down. The prophet can be momentarily blinded, but if the enemy blinds you, you will still be able to hear, smell, taste, and feel. If the enemy comes against your feelings, you'll still be able to see, hear, smell, and taste. A seer prophesies by all five senses, and so seers move in stronger discernment.

What does this look like? There may be times when you hear a prophecy, and a bad taste will come into your mouth. Your taste is discerning, *This isn't God.* But other times when you hear a prophecy, you'll start tasting gold. Whenever I taste gold, I know,

Man, that's it. I want to get all of this. God communicates with you through your senses.

It takes longer to become a mature seer than it does to become a mature prophet, because all five senses are involved. You have to learn how to discern your feelings, because there will be times when feelings come to you in ministry and they're not your feelings. And if you take them personally, you won't be active.

The one thing the Church has been taught against is feelings. But that's where you, as a seer, are the most accurate. You can take on how other people are feeling and know exactly how to minister to them. You can move right into their "living room" (their minds) and see what the problem is. You can feel what a person is feeling: depression, self-rejection, joy, anger, happiness. You can feel where they're coming from and then know exactly what to go for as you pray for them. So the seer is really strong in deliverance ministry.

The prophet can speak the future, but the seer can see what the people need to let go of in the past, tell them what the Lord is saying to them today, and declare what the Lord is offering them tomorrow. You can go right into their minds and see where the pain is coming from and what is still affecting and controlling their lives. Seers can help people forgive — usually themselves, help clean their minds out, and invite the Lord there.

Seers can knock on a person's front door, come in, and visit with that person without saying a word. A prophet can only prophesy as the faith arises. A lot of times, a prophet is just a person who really comes forth in faith, and that faith activates him so he can speak clearly. That is what Nathan the prophet was. He prophesied by the faith that rose in him. But a seer can have all five senses.

A seer can feel the strongholds of a town. If you enter a town and feel lust, lust owns that town. If you feel depression, it's a depressed place. As you come in there, you'll take on the feelings of that town, country, or person, whether they are good or bad. You'll know where there is self-rejection, because of what you feel. If you're ministering to somebody who has self-rejection, you'll feel it coming at yourself, and you must never take any of these things personally.

One of the strongest things to minister to is spirits of self-rejection. Suicidal spirits come through these spirits. A seer will feel these things. If you think they are coming from yourself, you will be totally unprofitable. So you need to have all these senses sanctified and be able to tell, *This is not me. I am not in self-rejection. I love myself. I can taste the Lord and see that He is good.*

You can also smell what's happening. You can discern what's wrong with a church or a city or even a nation, because you can smell it. You can smell sin, corruption, holiness. That's what 2 Corinthians 2:14 says: "But thanks be to God, who always leads us in triumph in Christ, and manifests through us the sweet aroma of the knowledge of Him in every place." So you can smell the sweet incense of the Lord. You can smell His presence when He comes out of people, for the kingdom is inside of us. You can actually smell when a person really yields to God.

You can discern what's going on with people through their incense. You can do it with your taste: "Taste and see that the Lord is good" (Psalm 34:8). You can do it through your feelings, through your sight, through the things you hear.

Seers are kicked out of a lot of churches, because you are the least understood of all the gifts. You are the one who feels like you don't fit any place except with other seers. Because of your revelation and dreams and the way God communicates with you, people think you're loony. But when churches reject you, they're bidding good-bye to their own mercy. As a seer, you are there for mercy. You are there to help bring healing to the people and show them what God is doing.

It is time for the seer to come forth. The Church needs you. It is time for the seer to mature and be used.

ACKNOWLEDGMENTS

To my wife for partnering with me on the wild ride of following God and sharing the cost for all of the successes and failures.

To my six children for provoking me to learn more of how God made me to function so I can help them find how God made them to function.

To my parents for leaving room for me to make my own decisions and follow God in my own way.

To Greg, Patty, Zach, Duncan, Sarah, and Anna Mapes for modeling a modern family directed by the unchanging hand of God and including me as one of their own.

To my editor, Lauren Stinton, for making the message of my heart coherent.

To Denton Presbyterian Church for providing a solid foundation in God and His Word that applies to all of Christian life, no matter the intensity of experience.

To John Paul Jackson for providing a rationale and a place to experiment with the seer gifting.

And most importantly, to Jesus for walking with me as I try to follow Him.

CHAPTER 1

WHAT IS A
SEER?

Intimate communion with God, where we hear His voice and see His face, is not reserved solely for life after death. It is for the here and now. He has created us to see Him, walk with Him, and interact with Him on a daily basis here on Earth. We bear His image, and the result is that we are incomplete without Him. We *need* interaction. We need to touch Him, to hear Him, to feel His heart, to taste His goodness, to smell His fragrance.

The seer gifting is an invitation from God to enter into the mystery of who He is. When I say "seer," I'm talking about people who go to seek relationship with God and find that He is speaking to them in all these different ways according to the five senses. I'll explain more of what that means in a moment.

First, as you begin this book, you should be aware that I am a Christian. I believe that God is Spirit and that He speaks to us, gives us pictures, releases visions and dreams, and pours out His spiritual gifts on people so that they will know Him and do His will. I believe the Bible is God's inspired Word and that everything it says is true. By stating this at the very beginning, I mean to articulate that if you are not a Christian, you could read this book and gain insight into what you are experiencing, but you won't be able to avoid the fact that everything in these pages is about God and how He formed the seer gifting to operate. That will be evident.

In order to begin to understand the seer gifting, we need to start with the basics. A seer is any person who has the ability to receive sensory input from the spiritual realm. This can happen at any level; we don't have to have experiences like Ezekiel in order to be a seer. In fact, many people are seers and don't realize it, usually because of one or more of three reasons:

1) No one has ever told them. *Maybe* they could relate some odd things that have happened to them, but no one has ever told them that what they're experiencing may not be "just their imagination." A lot of seers would say they have active imaginations or great intuition, and that's all. They don't realize it's more than that. Or, for example, they may see brief flashes of light or something move in their peripheral vision and assume it's just their eyes playing tricks on them, when they're actually seeing real flashes of light and real movement. They don't understand that these may be authentic. Similarly, they may walk into a room and get a feeling about

what is going on in the lives of the people present, but they think they are just guessing based on the people's posture and facial features.

2) Along similar lines, seers often don't realize that what they've been experiencing their entire lives is unique; they think everybody can do it. Or perhaps they suspect they are gifted in certain areas, but they don't realize that all the little things they keep dismissing are actually God trying to communicate with them and through them. For example, they may have detailed, extensive dreams; perhaps they've "known" things about people they just met or have been able to produce astounding works of art or make sound business decisions that have greatly impacted others. *I'm just good at what I do,* they may think. Or, *Can't everybody do this?*

3) Finally, some seers don't realize they're seers because as far back as they can remember, they seemingly have never done or experienced anything of a spiritual nature. Something shut the gifting down in them a long time ago, and at this point, they couldn't name even just one incident in which they knew God was talking to them. "He talks to other people," they say, "but He doesn't talk to me." Simply because it hasn't happened *yet* doesn't mean it can't or won't. We will be discussing this more later in the book.

WHAT IS SPIRITUAL SENSORY INPUT?

Here is what I mean by the term "sensory input." In the natural realm, we have our five senses that help us relate to the world and atmosphere around us. Through them we learn what things are, how they work, what's real, what something feels like, what it looks or tastes like, etc. They allow us to experience what is going on around us, and without them, we wouldn't be able to function. These form our physical sensory perceptions.

What are spiritual sensory perceptions? The Bible says that this world is a *type* of the world to come (1 Corinthians 15:44; Colossians 2:16–17; Romans 5:14). If what surrounds us now is just a reflection of the real, then imagine what the real must be like! Our natural five senses, therefore, reflect our spiritual senses, which are, by their very nature, better and stronger than what we know on Earth because they will continue to exist when our natural senses have ended.

As we think this through, we will be amazed at the implications. If we have any senses on Earth, we also have them in the spiritual realm, because that realm is the foundation of this one. As spiritual beings (Galatians 6:1; 1 Peter 2:5), we should be able to see, taste, smell, touch, and hear what is going on in the spiritual realm around us just as we can in the natural realm. At times, we will be able to smell what's in the spiritual air. We will see what is there to be seen, touch it, even taste it. We can describe it to others. We can *experience* the spiritual realm just as we can experience the natural realm.

These are our spiritual sensory perceptions, and we pick up on them in different ways. Sometimes, this information will come to us physically. For example, we may feel cold or hot when the natural temperature hasn't shifted a degree. This is happening because we're picking up on the spiritual "temperature" around us. At other times, we will receive spiritual information through our spiritual senses, which often feels like "just our imagination" and hence the reason many people don't realize they're gifted in this. Everyone has the capacity to experience the spiritual realm through the seer gifting, just as everyone has the capacity to hear God's voice.

For the sake of clarity, throughout this book we will often refer to all of the spiritual senses as "seeing" because all of them mean the same thing: We are picking up on spiritual sensory data — i.e., the realm of the spirit, which is the realm of God.

WHY IS THIS IMPORTANT?

How does this affect us, and why is it important to study this gifting? The writer of Hebrews says that the mature in Christ train their senses to discern what is God and what isn't (Hebrews 5:14). As we practice and study our giftings, we will mature in Him. We will grow in our knowledge of Him and His ways.

Again, this world is not our home; our home is Heaven — the spiritual realm — which automatically insinuates it is more important, more real and concrete, than this one. Because that's true, wouldn't we want to study it? Wouldn't we want to know more about it and see if there were any way we could learn to walk in it and be more affected by it now? Hand in hand with this is another reason that is even more important. As we study and grow in this gifting, we will be amazed at who God is, how intimate He desires to be with us, and how often He wants to communicate with us. We will fall further in love. We will be changed forever.

That is a very good reason.

God is with us, and studying our giftings and training ourselves in them will increase our realization of this, along with our faith. It will help us *see* His presence more and more.

WHAT IS THE PURPOSE OF THIS BOOK?

My goal in writing this book is to help you grow closer to Jesus. That is reason number one. Second, it is to encourage and equip you in your gifting and therefore help you change the world. If we are walking in the fullness of who we are, the Kingdom of God can't help but come into its fullness as well. If I can encourage you in your gifting, the purposes of Jesus will be that much more manifest in the Earth.

And finally, in writing this I want to encourage the Church, the downtrodden, and those who have lost hope to have hope once again. He has not passed you by. Studying this gifting within you will show you just how true that is.

CHAPTER 2

HOW DOES THE
SEER GIFTING FUNCTION?

In the first chapter of Jeremiah, God taught the young prophet how to use his seer gifting. This ancient reference is the modern-day key for seers who want to grow in their giftings:

> The word of the LORD came to me saying, "What do you see, Jeremiah?" And I said, "I see a rod of an almond tree."
>
> Then the LORD said to me, "You have seen well, for I am watching over My word to perform it."
>
> The word of the LORD came to me a second time saying, "What do you see?" And I said, "I see a boiling pot, facing away from the north."

29

> *Then the LORD said to me, "Out of the north the evil*
> *will break forth on all the inhabitants of the land."*
> — Jeremiah 1:11–14

In this passage, Jeremiah did three things. First, God came and prodded him to look for something. So Jeremiah looked. He opened his spiritual eyes and paid attention to what God was about to show him. Only then did he see. Something he had not noticed before was revealed to him, and he was able to tell God what it was. "I see a branch of an almond tree."

"Very good. Yes, you have seen an almond branch. Now this is what it means."

Jeremiah looked, he saw, and then he told God what he saw.

Looking and seeing is a common concept in Scripture. "'Seek, and you will find; knock, and it will be opened to you'" (Luke 11:9). Like Jeremiah, if we look for what God is showing us, we will see it; we will be able to receive what He is communicating to us and then seek to understand it.

Again, the seer gifting applies to everyone. Potentially all of us can see in the spiritual realm, and if we can't, something must have shut down the gifting. Perhaps someone in our family line refused to communicate with God this way, so the gifting is currently lying dormant within us. Perhaps we saw things that frightened us as children, and we tried to protect ourselves by shutting down in fear.

Not everyone is meant to be a seer at a highly public level, but everyone has the ability to receive sensory input from the spiritual realm.

How do we know if God means for us to explore this gifting and practice it? We know because we are interested in seeing. If we have that desire, God put it within us. Those of us who want to be chefs usually learn to cook more quickly than those who have no interest in cooking. In the same way, if we are interested in the seer gifting, it is for a reason, and we have the capacity to learn how to use it. It may or may not come easily to us, but if God has given us the desire to see, we can learn how to do so. If we have no desire to see, it won't bother us if we have trouble learning.

THREE TYPES OF SEEING

A few years ago, my grandmother died, and my family and I attended her funeral. During the service, my youngest at the time, Bekah, became confused about who had died. How could Grandma Barnes be dead? She was standing right there on stage. And she really was. Before Bekah said anything, in my spirit I had seen her there myself. We will discuss this story in greater detail later, but here, it serves as a good example of the different types of seeing.

When I see things, I typically see them one of two ways:

Internally: pictures in my mind that are similar to memories or thoughts

Externally: images that aren't really "there" in a physical sense (for example, seeing or sensing something on the kitchen table or across the room)

These two types of seeing are the more common types. They can come to us in relatively slight ways, so they seem like our imagination, or they can come more strongly. Sometimes, seers see external images so clearly and so strongly that they don't recognize that they're actually seeing in the spirit; to them, it seems like they are seeing physically. This was what my daughter Bekah experienced at the funeral. It seemed to her that her great-grandmother was actually standing there. I saw my grandmother in great detail, down to her hairstyle and the print on her shirt, but I recognized that I was seeing her in the spirit, while Bekah did not.

Finally, there is a third category of seeing: that of not being aware that you're seeing. People who gravitate toward this category don't believe they can see. They say things like:

"I wish I could see, but I can't."

"I don't do what you're talking about."

"God's gifted me in *other* areas."

In many cases, people who don't believe they are seers just haven't been able to step out in faith in this area. They assume that the thoughts, internal pictures, external images, and impressions God is giving them are just their imagination. Their hesitancy is usually because they don't think they are important enough to hear His voice, or they suppose that God speaks the way you and I speak: If He wants to get our attention, He'll tap us on the shoulder or shout our name from across the room. However, in most people's experiences with God, that is *rarely* what happens. Instead, He seems to communicate most often in a whisper, something that can be overlooked if we're not paying attention.

Here is an odd thing about the people who believe they

are part of this final category. I've discovered that those who "don't see" potentially can see more clearly than I can! They simply haven't been able to accept that they are seeing. Again, this is true for all the spiritual senses. For example, we may feel a tangible sensation of approaching danger but dismiss it as worry.

THE PRICE OF THE GIFTING

As I wrote in the last chapter, one of the purposes of this book is to help you realize that God is speaking to you through the things you see, hear, and experience with your spiritual senses. Another purpose is to help you understand those things. I want to help you understand and use your gifting, because I know that some of you, like myself, have spent years feeling abnormal, alone, and that no one understood you. Every gifting, spiritual or natural, has a cost. Most require years of study and training; some require solitude and temporary separation from family

> WHEN WE UNDERSTAND THE SEER GIFTING, THE COST WE'VE PAID FOR IT BECOMES A FORCE THAT PROPELS US INTO OUR DESTINIES.

and community. The seer gifting comes with a price as well, and if you're going to pay that price, as some of you already have, you also need to reap the benefit of it; otherwise, you will lose your hope.

When we understand the seer gifting, the cost we've paid for it becomes a force that propels us into our destinies. Decades of misunderstanding and rejection blow away in an instant when we finally understand why we're made the way we're made and what God has called us to do. When understanding comes, hope comes as well, and wounded hearts can exclaim, *Oh, wow! This was worth it.* We'll be talking about this more as the book progresses.

METAPHORICAL UNDERSTANDING

As we begin to explore the seer gifting, we are quickly met with a realization: It is one thing to realize that we're hearing from God; it is quite another to understand what He is saying.

God will sometimes communicate with words or pictures that have a literal meaning. He will give people visions of actual future events that could happen just as they appeared to them. He may tell someone, "Don't take this route on your way home." Or, "Your car is going to run out of gas this afternoon." But He doesn't always speak that way.

In Scripture, He took ideas, actions, and objects the Israelites commonly understood and used them to describe His nature. He revealed Himself through dreams, metaphors, riddles, hidden meanings, and other things that required relationship with Him, revelation, time, and perseverance in order to understand:

> He shall cover you with His feathers,
> And under His wings you shall take refuge.
> — Psalm 91:4, NKJV

> "When anyone hears the word of the kingdom and does not understand it, the evil one comes and snatches away what has been sown in his heart. This

is the one on whom seed was sown beside the road."
— Matthew 13:19

*And I saw between the throne (with the four living
creatures) and the elders a Lamb standing, as if slain,
having seven horns and seven eyes, which are the
seven Spirits of God, sent out into all the earth.*
— Revelation 5:6

These are but a few examples of God's metaphorical language as seen in the words He uses and how He made certain things to exist. There are many, many more examples in Scripture — including the ancient Hebrew language itself, as we will discuss in Chapter Eight.

Many people refer to God's metaphorical language as "dark speech." *Dark* doesn't always have a negative connotation; it can also mean something that isn't clearly visible — that is, something we have to study, meditate on, and spend time with before we come into a deeper understanding of it. The Bible uses "dark" in several passages to describe what God is doing, where He is, or in reference to something not easily understood:

*So the people stood afar off, but Moses drew near the
thick darkness where God was.*
— Exodus 20:21, NKJV

*"I will give you the treasures of darkness
And hidden wealth of secret places,*

So that you may know that it is I,
The LORD, the God of Israel, who calls you by your name."
— Isaiah 45:3

When something is *dark*, we will be able to understand it only when *light* comes and shines on it: when God gives us revelation.

Do you see this? He asks quietly. *What I'm showing you right now is like Me, and when you understand the similarity, you will understand Me in a greater way.*

Without the Holy Spirit's guidance, we won't successfully bridge the gap between what God is revealing to us (the object, picture, impression, etc.) and what it means. That being the case, two principal things are required in order to begin to understand God's metaphorical language: relationship with Him, which is what everything in life boils down to, and the disciplined use of our giftings.

RELATIONSHIP WITH GOD AND UNDERSTANDING METAPHORS

Whenever God communicates through metaphors and other forms of dark speech, He's provoking us to learn His language. He's inviting us to think and act as He thinks and acts, so that we can understand Him better and come into deeper relationship with Him. The imagery God uses isn't an attempt to keep us at arm's length; it is an effort to help us *see* Him. In that specific moment, nothing else would work as well to show us who He is.

By spending time with Him and cultivating friendship with

Him, we begin to understand why He does what He does and why He says what He says. Our relationship then deepens. The outcome of intimacy with Him is that we grow to be like Him. We begin to love the way He loves and to see ourselves the way He sees us. His proximity initiates greater anointing in our lives, which causes our metaphorical understanding to grow.

SELF-DISCIPLINE AND UNDERSTANDING METAPHORS

To build our metaphorical understanding, we first need relationship with God. Second, we need to discipline ourselves to learn to think metaphorically. When God shows us something, we should be in the habit of immediately asking, *What does this represent?* Did the object appear in Scripture? If so, what did it represent there? How did Jesus interpret the parables? Why did He say that seeds represent the spoken word of God? How did Joseph know that three branches stood for three days in the cupbearer's dream? These are interpretative models for us to follow.

> THE OUTCOME OF INTIMACY WITH HIM IS THAT WE GROW TO BE LIKE HIM.

Christian dream dictionaries[1] are sometimes helpful in this process, because they have done a portion of this research already. Keep in mind, however, that the meanings, or significance, of metaphors may change depending on the context, situation, and what God wants to tell you specifically. For instance, God sometimes represents Himself with fire (Exodus 3), but at other

---

1   See the Bibliography and Suggested Resources at the back of this book.

times, He represents Himself with a lamb (Revelation 5:11–12). He shows different aspects of Himself at different times. Fire does not always represent God in Scripture. Sometimes, it represents judgment (Revelation 20:10). If God shows you a picture involving fire, obviously, it would be important to know what He wants the fire to represent in that instance! Is He bringing judgment, or is He doing something else?

Discipline is important because in order for anything to make sense, it needs to align with our existing understanding in some way. When we're looking for something that makes a level of sense to us, our brain can put two and two together more easily. This is called pattern recognition. If we know what something *could* mean, we are more open to God giving us understanding.

The issue that automatically arises with this is that when we're looking for something that makes sense to us, our minds filter out whatever doesn't make sense. And as many of us have experienced, God can be *difficult* to understand. This is why discipline is important; it is the bridge to revelation. It gives us a foundation. We know what something *could* mean, and we wait for God to confirm it to us.

Without disciplined metaphorical understanding, we may have a hard time comprehending what we're receiving from the spiritual realm. If we do manage to stumble across the right interpretation, we won't really know how we got there or how to get there again in the future. When we are disciplined, we can take the word, picture, impression, or other communication; bring it close to what we *think* it could mean; and then wait for the Holy Spirit's confirmation — His spark — to speak to our hearts and show us that we have the right interpretation.

Revelation without discipline means that we may receive a genuine prophecy from God, but we don't wait to confirm with Him the word's timing, nature, or whether or not He wants us to repeat it. Those who listen to our words may feel the Holy Spirit's anointing on them and be able to tell that God said *something*, but most likely, they will not be as impacted as they would have been if we had taken the time to wait. Or worse, they may think God said something He didn't.

On the other hand, if we are too focused on discipline, we will attempt to sew together a prophetic word or an interpretation that seems godly, but it has no spark — no life in it.

Many of us have a hard time balancing revelation and discipline. We feel as if we're letting go of one to grab the other, but this isn't the case. When we know what metaphors commonly mean (discipline), it is as if we can draw dots on the page and then wait for God to connect them for us (revelation). When the connection occurs, we sense in our spirits, *Yes, this is what that means.*

Once while teaching a class, I saw a bronze snake wrapped around a woman's head. I knew from studying metaphors that snakes typically represent deception. Based on that alone, it could have been very simple for me to assume something potentially negative about this woman. *The snake is around her head, so it must be that she has been deceived in some area of her thinking.*

However, bronze is a substance that has been tested in fire. In Ezekiel 1, the creature he described had burnished bronze feet so that it could stand in the fire and not melt or break. Also in the Old Testament, the Israelites raised up a bronze snake in the wilderness to bring healing. In the Gospels, Jesus said that we need to be as innocent as doves and as wise as serpents, so apparently, a snake can sometimes mean wisdom as well.

Untested wisdom allows for deception; Eve listened to some untested wisdom from a serpent in the Garden. But if we test wisdom, it becomes bronze: something hard and strong that won't fall apart. I waited for the Holy Spirit's confirmation, and when I sensed it, I was able to tell this woman that God had been refining the wisdom in her bloodline. There had been some deception in her grandfathers, but God had refined the wisdom within her and had made her like burnished bronze. He had given her the wisdom of God.

That is the moment of metaphorical understanding — it comes with the spark. If we don't sense the Spirit's confirmation, the object or activity probably means something other than what we thought it meant. Every time I know of when I have been wrong in an interpretation, it was because I didn't wait for God to confirm the meaning in my spirit. The danger with having success in metaphorical understanding is not waiting. It takes a good deal of peace to sit with God and let Him say whatever He wants to say, despite what we think or feel and despite what the metaphor logically seems to suggest to our natural minds.

> To BUILD OUR METAPHORICAL UNDERSTANDING, WE FIRST NEED RELATIONSHIP WITH GOD.

Without His guidance, we will find ourselves relying on our assumptions. If we're overly optimistic in nature, we'll be prone to assume that everything we see is positive, when something could be corrective. If we're overly pessimistic, we'll tend to think everything we see is negative and therefore may have a hard time accurately revealing the Father's heart to those around us.

There is a moment when we're looking for metaphorical understanding and we let go of all our preconceptions. At that moment, it feels like we have no idea what we're doing. We don't have a clue what God is going to tell us about what we're seeing, but based on our history with Him, we know He's going to tell us something. In that moment of being completely open, we experience great growth, because that is when we experience the spark.

DISCERNMENT: THE SEER'S LIFELINE

What is one of the results of growing close to God and being disciplined in our giftings? The result is discernment, which enables us to tell the difference between God's voice, our own thoughts, and the voice of the enemy.

A few years ago, I was going through a time in which I was seeing a lot of angels. They would often give me objects or have messages from God, His assignments for me, and other things. One day, while I was sitting in an airport and waiting to board my connecting flight, I saw an angel quite clearly — not with my physical eyes, but I had a very strong awareness of him over my right shoulder. He held out a manila envelope and said, "This is your assignment for where you're going."

As I went to grab it, it occurred to me that this angel might not be from God. I sensed that something wasn't quite right. Hesitating, I asked, "Who is Jesus to you?" (See 1 John 4:1.)

He said, "Um," a few times and then disappeared.

I was very glad it had occurred to me to validate the source of that angel. God hadn't sent him. He would have given me a counterfeit assignment, which, no doubt, would have negatively affected my trip.

Relationship and history with God develop our discernment: a sensitivity to the Spirit that enables us to recognize His voice. This is important because His voice, as well as the enemy's voice, can sound a lot like our own thoughts. For example, we could think, *Bill has been on my mind a lot lately. Every time I think about him, I feel stress. Maybe I should pray for him.* That is an example of an "everyday" thought that could be of God but sounds like something that might just pass through our minds. This next thought also sounds somewhat normal but could be coming from the enemy: *Why doesn't the pastor realize how gifted I am? I feel overlooked. He must not be listening to God.* Discernment helps us recognize the source.

When God has built up within us a sensitivity to His Holy Spirit, we will be more able to tell when something is amiss with our thoughts, emotions, plans, and interactions with others, as well as when He is highlighting something, speaking to us, nudging our hearts, or quietly showing us His truth.

Discernment is the seer's lifeline. Cults and religious factions are sometimes the byproduct of sincere, gifted, faith-filled Christian leaders who believe they're doing what God has told them to do. We should never stop praying for discernment, because it will keep us from confusing God's voice with any other voice. It will keep us out of the New Age and witchcraft. The New

Age movement is filled with revelatory seers, but they have very little relationship with God, so they can't understand the source of what they're seeing. Many of them genuinely desire to follow truth, but they are not able to discern between light from God and what is only pretending to be light.

Once God has developed discernment within us, we can be trusted to see more and more, because now we can recognize what we're seeing, and He knows we will act wisely. Practicing discernment leads to greater discernment. Like faith, the more we use our discernment, the greater it becomes.

God's process of growing us in this area is similar to how a dad would teach his little girl to ride a bicycle. He attaches the training wheels and then pushes his daughter along until she learns how to balance, steer, and avoid obstacles. After a while, the training wheels are removed. The dad again helps guide the bike and then slowly releases it as she learns how to ride on her own.

As we are able and ready, God puts the weight of discernment on us. He gives us the opportunity to make bad decisions because He knows we're now able to *not* make them. He grows discernment within us and only afterward puts us in situations where we'll have to use it. In the story I just told you, I had been interacting with angels, and God had protected me from interacting with anything that wasn't from Him. Now He was allowing something negative to approach me, because He knew there would be a check in my spirit that asked, *Wait a minute — is this God?*

In Exodus 32 when God told Moses that He was going to destroy the Israelites, He knew how Moses would react; He knew the Israelites were going to live. He had lent Moses His attributes of mercy and love, and He knew that Moses was going to seek His favor on the people's behalf.

In my experience, God won't allow us to enter situations that are dangerous for us until we're capable of choosing wisely. He is just; when He tests us, He wants us to succeed, not to fail. When He made Saul king of Israel, Saul had the capability of being successful. He could have been a great and godly king, but he *chose* not to be. Knowing the future, God planned on using his failure, but He didn't make it impossible for Saul to succeed.

Having discernment doesn't mean that we're incapable of making poor decisions. Like Saul, we could choose to ignore God's still, small voice within us, or we could purposefully put ourselves into situations that are over our heads. There is always the possibility for failure because without it, our success wouldn't have real meaning.

It is humbling to realize that we're capable of failing. After we've made a right decision, God will sometimes show us how easily we could have made the wrong decision, and we're filled with gratitude and thankfulness. In His grace, He kept us from failing.

Discernment will come as a result of relationship with God. The two form a circle; as we grow in discernment, we will also grow in our relationship with Him.

PROPHETIC & SEER Q&A:

In the Prophetic & Seer Q&A area of www.stirthewater.com, users can submit questions about the seer gifting: what they've seen, their concerns, their frustrations, how they could improve, what they should do with what they're seeing, etc. The question below was submitted on the Stir the Water site.

QUESTION: Just wondering what you might suggest for people who have received prophetic words about the future on many, many occasions and had all the words fall away as false? Some words being from very "high" up spiritual leaders. Would it be that people who only ever get wrong words are only interpreting what others see for them incorrectly, or is there something more to it? And if they are always just interpreting what is being seen for them incorrectly, how would they correct their understanding?

ANSWER: Here are four things I believe we need to keep in mind whenever someone gives us a revelatory or prophetic word.

SEEK CONFIRMATION FROM GOD

First of all, we need to hear from God for ourselves on a consistent basis. Depending on what we're going through, this can be difficult. We can go through days or seasons of turmoil, when it's very difficult to hear from God because we don't have enough peace.

But here's the reason this is important: If we're consistently hearing from God for ourselves, then what He has told us in our alone times with Him will confirm what we're hearing from other people.

This doesn't require high, clear, awesome revelation; we just need to go to God on a daily basis. Even if all we "hear" or sense is vague, and we're not quite sure what He said or if He said anything, over time this builds up within us a fairly high level of confirmation. We will sense our spirits bearing witness to the word. It isn't just our minds saying, *Oh, I like that. That would be nice.* Instead, it feels as if our spirits are saying, *Yes! Yes!*

Every time we receive a word, we should seek God for confirmation. Always. The confirmation may come beforehand, right afterward, in one clear moment or subtly over time. It may happen in a moment or be spread out over several days.

DISTINGUISH BETWEEN POTENTIAL AND ESTABLISHED OUTCOMES

Now, that being said, there may be times when we know a word has been confirmed, but it still doesn't come to pass. The probable reason for this is that the word was about a *potential* outcome and not an *established-by-God* outcome. There's a difference.

For example, let's say that Alice is called to live in Africa as a missionary, but she chooses not to go. The potential is there, but she doesn't step into it, so it doesn't happen. Or perhaps she wants to go, but her husband doesn't, and so the word doesn't come to pass because of someone else's choice. In some cases, a word that does or doesn't come to pass may not have anything to do with the person who received it. It may be solely dependent on outside sources.

Revelatory words can be about something that has potential and is later realized, or they can be about something that God has already established. The latter is a high-level revelation about what God is going to do. He has *chosen* for such-and-such to happen. The choices involved have already been made; the cost has already been paid, and it's going to happen. A revelatory word about something with potential isn't a false word; it is simply an outcome that may or may not be realized.

This agrees with what Jesus said in Matthew 22:14: Many are called, but few are chosen. I think that statement is true of almost every potentiality in creation. Many things are called to come to pass, but few things are actually chosen to come to pass.

Distinguishing between a potential outcome and a chosen outcome can be difficult for revelatory people, especially if they don't understand the dynamic or don't have clarity or discernment. It can also be hard if they're trying to sound more certain than they feel. God could be saying, "I am calling this to happen," and the person assumes that means, "God says this is *going* to happen."

Again, connecting this with the previous point, we need to pray about every word we receive, from anyone. We need to ask God, "Is this established? Or is this still just a possibility?" That dynamic is huge.

RECOGNIZE ISSUES OF TIMING AND METAPHOR

Long before they come to pass, many prophecies seem like they're never going to. Some of us wait months and years and then conclude all of those words must have been false. But then another ten years go by, and we start realizing, "Wait a second. They're *all* happening."

Timing is vital. Revelatory words are often given without a clear sense of timing, and we tend to assume that if God said something today, it must be about today. But often, that is not the case. When we seek God for confirmation about a word, we should also seek confirmation about the timing.

Finally, a revelatory word can be so metaphoric that it seems to mean one thing but actually means something else. It was a good word, but we assumed it must have been false because the way it played out didn't look the way we expected. That is often the case as well.

WHAT CAN WE DO?

All of the above can be issues. In summation, we first need to be in the habit of spending time with God, because then, when someone gives us a genuine word from Him, we will have an internal witness.

Second, we should ask God if the word is about an established or potential outcome. Maybe we need to pray into it. Maybe we need to wait. Maybe we just need to know that it *could* happen, but it's based on other people's faith and choices.

Finally, there is also the issue of waiting for God's perfect timing, as well as understanding the metaphor and being certain we really do know what He means.

At any given time, we could be dealing with one or several of these four issues. We could be in a season in which nothing seems to be working, and we're tempted to think all our revelatory words are false. But that may not be the case. It could be that they just didn't happen the way we expected them to happen. It could be that they haven't happened *yet*.

If you're in a season like that and feel discouraged, know that it won't last forever. You will also go through seasons in which all the words you receive are right on. All the timing is right. Your understanding is right, and the words aren't potential outcomes that *could* happen — they are established by God, and you are able to watch them unfold.

All these things require discernment, experience, patience and grace. We need to keep them in mind and seek God on them whenever we are given a prophetic word.

CHAPTER 3

THE BEGINNER'S GUIDE TO PAYING ATTENTION

Several years ago, my wife, Mims, and I drove out to California. During the trip, we had some car trouble, and she went to the home of a woman we had just met while I stayed behind to get the car fixed.

After they had gone, I realized I had misplaced the directions. I had never been to this city before. I didn't know where our new friend lived. I didn't have her phone number, and neither Mims nor I had a cell phone. I had a vague recollection of the directions our friend had told me, and that was it.

After the car was fixed, I drove around for hours, trying to find my wife and remember the directions to our friend's home. I kept driving past a nice apartment complex, and every time, I felt an urge to stop. *That would be a great place to go*, I thought. I wanted to check it out, but it didn't fit the directions I remembered, so I ignored it and kept driving. And driving. And driving.

Finally, I gave up and thought, *I'm going to check this place out.* So I went to the apartment complex, and to my surprise, it turned out to be exactly where I was supposed to go. Our friend lived there.

The voice of God has a way of sneaking up on us. It can feel so natural to us, so much like our own thought processes, that we automatically dismiss it. There are also times when God speaks to us, and the idea, picture, impression, word, or whatever else He puts in our heads seems imprudent or even foolish to us. For instance, why would I have wanted to stop at that apartment complex? I *knew* it wasn't where I was supposed to go. But God put a strong desire in me to stop and check it out. He was directing me, and I didn't realize it until afterward.

It takes time to begin to recognize God's voice and stop brushing it aside. My wife and I have six children. As you can imagine, through the years, I've had plenty of practice conversing with excited, grunting, squealing kids, and like many fathers, I've discovered that little storytellers can be difficult to understand.

As we grow up, we are trained to focus on logic — that which makes the most sense to us. Listening to young children can be hard because it forces our brains to process information in ways we haven't been trained in. We don't immediately recognize what many small children are trying to say.

One of the keys to seeing in the spiritual realm is relearning how to think and process information. Children tend to pick up on a great deal more of the spiritual realm than adults do, because they haven't learned to tune it out. They pay attention to what they're thinking and feeling even if those things are not explainable. They are fully convinced there is a monster under the bed or hiding in the closet. They have made-up friends and conversations. They play all the time. We assume "they're just being kids" and dismiss their fantastic stories, because we *know* there isn't anything under the bed or hiding in the closet. We *know* the games they make up are just games and nothing of a deeper origin. So we dismiss their stories and don't realize how easy it is to do the same thing with the Holy Spirit and what He is communicating to us.

Jesus said we need to come to Him like little children (Matthew 18:2–5). In the last chapter, we talked about the importance of having discipline *and* revelation. Little children don't have much of the former at all. They are in the process of learning, but they aren't "trained" yet. Training can be highly beneficial and necessary; it prepares us for future events, disciplines us in the proper use of our giftings, gives us context, and

> ONE OF THE KEYS TO SEEING IN THE SPIRITUAL REALM IS RELEARNING HOW TO THINK AND PROCESS INFORMATION.

helps us understand what we're doing and why. However, if there isn't room for the Spirit of God to come in and show Himself to be bigger than anything we've imagined, we can train ourselves into a stalemate. Many of us have spent years in the stalemate stage.

It takes time, but just as we can train ourselves to ignore the spiritual activity constantly surrounding us, we can also train ourselves to pay attention to it.

In this chapter, we will be going over the steps we can take to learn to stop ourselves from ignoring or overlooking sensory input from the spiritual realm.

STEP ONE:
START PAYING ATTENTION TO
THE THINGS THAT DON'T MAKE SENSE

Typically, when I first perceive something in the spiritual realm, I don't have any idea what it means. This has been happening more frequently with time. The more I understand of God and His ways, the more I realize how much I don't understand. True mystery becomes *more* mysterious the closer we get to its source, not less.

How do we learn to pay attention to the thoughts, feelings, pictures, images, etc. that don't easily make sense? First, we deliberately seek out metaphorical understanding. We do this by asking God to show us something we don't understand and then asking Him to explain it, as He did for Jeremiah in Jeremiah 1. We don't need to do this for long periods of time every day; we just need to do it consistently. This will train us to think metaphorically, and it will also train us to be more aware of His voice, His movements, the quiet impressions He puts within us, the pictures He shows us, and every other way He may communicate with us.

As we grow in intimacy with God, we increase in our ability to receive revelation. Revelation increases intimacy, and likewise, intimacy increases revelation. Therefore, the most important thing we could do to grow in relationship with Him is spend time with Him, listening to His voice and paying attention to what He shows us, even if we have no understanding of what the picture or object means. For most of us, this is no easy task, and as contrary as it sounds, listening to Jesus for yourself is especially hard if you're in full-time ministry.

There was a season in my life when I would teach a few classes, speak at different churches, and suddenly realize that I hadn't listened to God outside of ministering to other people in six months, simply because I'd been doing my job. I had a horrible time making myself sit down, take a few minutes, and just interact with Him. I became so desperate that I actually put a "Spend Time with God and Listen" chart on the back of my office door, and I'd mark the days I did it. I felt like a little kid putting stars on the calendar, but if I wasn't that meticulous, I wouldn't do it.

STEP TWO:
EVALUATE WHAT GOD SEEMS TO BE SAYING

Each of us is different in how we receive and process information. Math is a good example of this; not all of us enjoy working with numbers, but that doesn't mean it's impossible for us. It may just take us a little longer to work the problems.

Certain people will find that they're gifted in metaphorical understanding. They seem to have a sixth sense that enables them to understand what they're seeing or sensing. Most of us, however, will experience this infrequently. Sometimes we may understand what God is showing us right away, but often, we will start off with a slight understanding that grows with time and perseverance. The interpretation could come in only a few minutes, or it could come days or even months later. At times, I have been involved in a task seemingly unrelated to the picture He showed me, and suddenly,

He connected the dots, and I realized what He was trying to tell me. It takes discernment to be able to know what He's saying, when He's saying it, and what our response to His words should be.

There are a few simple steps that can help this process flow more smoothly:

WAIT FOR GOD

We discussed the importance of waiting for the Holy Spirit's spark in the last chapter. Once we have seen, sensed, or otherwise experienced something we don't understand, we need to pause. We need to take a moment, quiet ourselves, and wait for the Spirit of God to breathe the answer into our hearts. He may do this through a thought, a memory, a feeling, or another picture. He may bring a Scripture to mind. The meaning could be based on what the metaphor has meant in the past, or it could mean something new and different that has never occurred to us before. Again, waiting for the spark is vital to receiving and understanding revelation.

> NO MATTER OUR GIFTING, ONE OF THE MOST IMPORTANT THINGS WE CAN DO IS ASK GOD OUR QUESTIONS AND EXPECT HIM TO ANSWER US.

ASK GOD FOR CLARIFICATION

No matter our gifting, one of the most important things we can do is ask God our questions and expect Him to answer us. This is such a simple, childlike response that many of us overlook it because we're bracing ourselves for something more difficult.

However, when we buy something at a store and we can't

get it to work, we consult the manufacturer. God wants to interact with us, with big things and with small things. He gave us that word or picture; He spoke it into our spirits. It started with Him, so if we don't understand it, we can take it back to Him and say, "What did You mean with this? You gave it to me, but I don't know how it works."

PRAY ABOUT IT

Finally, if God has shown us something and we don't know what it means or how to respond, we can pray about it. We can return it to Him in prayer, and He will still move according to what He has shown us. He honors the prayer even though our understanding isn't complete.

STEP THREE:
REALIZE THAT GOD CAN SPEAK THROUGH ANYTHING

As God grows our discernment, we begin to realize how much He actually speaks to us. This causes us to be more receptive to hearing from Him everywhere we go and in every situation we find ourselves in.

Could God speak to us through our three-year-old daughter who doesn't want to go to bed? Yes. Could He speak to us through someone who is obviously operating out of the soul — meaning, from his or her own selfish motivations? Yes. God could speak to us through *anything*: something we haven't thought about in years, a commercial on television, a movie, a song on the radio, a billboard we pass on the road, a sense or feeling, a coworker's offhand remark. The more sensitive we are to the Spirit of God, the more we'll recognize the Holy Spirit's spark within us.

Having discernment also enables us to recognize God's voice when He says something we're not expecting to hear, when we're not expecting to hear it. A few years ago, I was having lunch with John Paul Jackson (founder of Streams Ministries International) and three other men, one of whom we'll call Bill. The pastor thought Bill was really prophetic and that it would be good for him to talk to John Paul, because, as it often is with highly gifted people, there was no one else for him to talk to. And that became very evident the longer we sat with him. For an hour and a half, Bill never paused to take a breath. He asked John Paul a hundred questions and then didn't give him any time to respond.

Sitting there, I thought, *What is this guy doing? Doesn't he realize that a lot of people would love to have an hour and a half with John Paul? He won't let him say a word.*

I was offended on John Paul's behalf and wondered if I should say something to Bill about it. Bill finally left, and as we were walking back to the car, John Paul turned to us.

"I've learned that God will speak to me through anybody," he said. "Even though that guy was sitting there babbling, God spoke a few things to me. People need to be listened to and affirmed that they really do hear from Him if they're to grow and reach their destiny."

I was convicted. I had been irritated and annoyed, and John Paul had been listening — really listening, not just nodding his head at the appropriate moments. He'd been paying attention, and he'd heard God's voice.

Very rarely is God not communicating. Consequently, when we want to interact with Him, but we don't feel successful, it may be that He wants to address something we're not open to talking about; we may not be paying attention to the idea He wants to discuss. For example, if we're not expecting a surprise party for our birthday, we may not notice the suspicious way our spouse is acting. However, if we are expecting one, we will notice his or her "odd" behavior right away. We will find what we search for (Luke 11:9).

When we learn to "think openly," even regarding things that don't make sense or seem beyond the realm of possibility, we will experience greater and greater revelation. Being childlike this way allows God to take our hands and lead us where He wants to go. It allows us to better see Him as He is and causes us not to restrict our interactions to our preconceived ideas of Him.

PROPHETIC & SEER Q&A:

QUESTION: Does it take awhile sometimes before a person can see? Also does it matter if my eyes are opened or closed? Can anyone have this gift? Or is it only some people who can become prophetic/seers?

ANSWER: This is a very large topic, and to answer it as completely as possible, we would need much more space than we have here. So this will be a "short" answer, not a comprehensive one.

Potentially everyone can see. When we can't see, it could be for a few different reasons: Our gifting is dormant, we aren't ready to see yet, we don't realize we already are seeing (that the pictures in our heads are from God), something in our bloodline (like a spiritual curse) is keeping our gifts from functioning, or the enemy made us fearful of our giftings when we were young and we responded by shutting them down.

If you have ever asked God to take away your seeing gift, you may need to repent now if you want to begin to see again. We need to repent whenever we reject what He has given us, whether that be seeing, hearing, singing, writing, playing the piano, painting, running — anything. Repentance tells our spirit to do things according to God's ways and stop doing things the way we have been.

Not everyone is meant to be a seer at a highly public level, like Ezekiel was, but potentially everyone can see. As we begin to explore this gifting, what God communicates to us often feels like just our imagination, but as He builds our discernment, we'll be able to recognize more easily what is from Him and what genuinely is "just us."

How do we know if we are meant to see? We know because we're interested in seeing. If we want to see, we have the capacity to learn. It may or may not come easily to us, but if God has given us the interest and desire to see, we can learn to do so. If we have no desire to see, it won't bother us if we have trouble seeing.

Seeing spiritual things with our spiritual eyes is usually easier to do than seeing with our "eyes open," or with our physical eyes. That can be a bigger door to walk through. To do that, some of us may need a "breakthrough" moment, such as being in a place where God is doing things and there is a lot of anointing. This could be at church or a prophetic conference or something similar.

People who do the "Eyes Wide Open" exercise on stirthewater.com often say they don't see anything in the beginning, but they see something later in the exercise or when they're doing the exercise again, and they realize they actually were seeing things their whole lives and never knew it.

CHAPTER 4

WHY DOES IT FEEL LIKE I'M MAKING IT UP?

The question in this chapter title comes up again and again on www.stirthewater.com[1] and whenever I teach on the seer gifting.

"I don't feel like I'm getting anything from God," people will tell me. "I feel like I'm making this up."

When I ask them what they're "making up," they usually tell me something that is obviously from God, but the subtle, everyday way it came to them suggested it couldn't be anything but their imagination. They thought they were making something up, when they were actually picking up on what the Holy Spirit was showing them and they just didn't realize it.

In an attempt to explain how this works, I frequently tell people that their revelator is right next to their maker-upper,

---

1 For more information about www.stirthewater.com, see Appendix 1.

meaning that in the beginning, it often feels like we're "making it up" because God is communicating with us through our imagination. Why else would we have an imagination? Would He have given us one if He hadn't intended to use it Himself? I believe that the *primary* function of the imagination is for us to conceive of what God is communicating.

The Apostle Paul wrote that God is beyond anything we could ever ask for or *imagine* (Ephesians 3:16–21). He is far beyond what we as humans can easily understand, so when He speaks of Himself, He's telling us what we don't yet comprehend and often what we haven't yet experienced (Romans 4:17). Following the logical progression, therefore, if we haven't experienced something yet, how can we begin to understand it? How can we even picture what it is? We have to *imagine* what God is saying for us to actually *hear* what He's saying. This is what artistically minded people and analytically minded people do every time they conceive of a new idea. They have to imagine what it will look like in order to understand it and then carry it out.

Our revelator is next to our maker-upper. Are we making it up? Maybe not. It could be coming from outside of us. Does it feel like we're making it up? Often, yes, because our minds are trying to make sense of a new idea.

My wife and I used to teach teenagers at a summer family camp how to hear God's voice. One year, one of the girls told me that she didn't believe God spoke to anybody. After we gave her a word the first night, she changed her mind.

"I believe God spoke through you guys," she said, but she didn't believe that God would speak through her peers.

Later, we practiced hearing God's voice as a group, and some of the kids gave words to one another. After that, she said, "Okay, so God speaks through them, too, but He doesn't speak through me."

The next exercise didn't change her mind.

"I'm not getting anything here," she said.

"Make something up," I told her.

So she made something up, and it was incredible. She gave an accurate word of knowledge about some hard, painful things another girl in the group had experienced. She was exceptionally accurate, and all she'd done was "make something up."

If you aren't in the habit of utilizing your imagination, using your seer gifting could be harder for you at the beginning than it is for others. But no matter your level of experience, this is a growing process; you will find yourself accurate in certain areas and truly "making stuff up" in other areas. However, the more you practice, the better you'll become at discerning when it's just you and when you're actually receiving information from God. You may be surprised at how often it is the latter.

When I was a teenager, I would get frustrated whenever I'd spend time with God. *I'm not hearing from You! All I'm getting are these little pictures.* It took some time, but I finally realized that all those little pictures *were* my hearing from Him. He'd been speaking to me and showing me Himself all along, and I was trying to ignore what was coming to mind, because I thought it was the result of a hyperactive imagination.

Perhaps you're in the middle of wrestling with this issue as well. Automatically assuming something is "just you" is a mistake.

Even if a large portion of what you're seeing right now is "just you," as you practice hearing from God, He will draw near you, and your discernment will increase. You'll get better at distinguishing the source of what you're experiencing, and you'll consequently begin to receive more of God's communications.

Instead of asking, *Did I make that up?* It is much better to ask, *God, was that You?* The latter question removes the focus off ourselves and allows room for Him to show us that yes, it was Him, or no, He was actually saying this other thing. Typically, understanding won't be able to come if we're stuck between *How do I know that was God?* and *Did I just make that up?*

Paying attention to our imagination is vital if we want to communicate with God, because when He has given us something (a sense, a picture, or anything else), it sits there inside of us until we deal with it — i.e., accept it as being of God, even if we don't yet understand what it means. If it remains inside of us, ignored or disregarded, over time it will get in the way and clog our system, like buildup in a garbage disposal or an unhealthy amount of cholesterol in our arteries. Even slight amounts of

> " INSTEAD OF ASKING, DID I MAKE THAT UP? IT IS MUCH BETTER TO ASK, GOD, WAS THAT YOU? "

revelation will begin this process, so imagine what a person's soul must look like after he or she has spent *years* stuffing down and ignoring all the things God was communicating!

What God has deposited in our spirits will prod at us until we do something about it. We may begin to feel restless and not know why; we may feel like something is missing and has been missing for so long that we can't remember what it was or how to get it back. We can remove the "clog" by acknowledging what He's put within us — by drawing it out on paper, talking about it, meditating on it, praying about it. We honor Him by recording what we sense He's telling or showing us and then asking, "God, is this You?" Only then will we relieve the pressure building in our spirits. When the pipe is washed clean, we will be able to hear, see, and experience the spiritual realm much more clearly.

As we discussed at the beginning of Chapter Two, God taught Jeremiah to see using a three-step process. First, he was to look. Then, because he looked, he was able to see, and finally, he needed to admit what he saw. By admitting what we think we're seeing — saying it out loud, writing it down, or communicating it through some other method — we allow it to move from what we think we *might have heard* to something that God actually showed us. It escalates the revelation, strengthens our senses, and reinforces our faith that we do hear from Him. If in the process we discover that what we thought might have been God really wasn't God, we can simply dismiss it.

As seers, it is very important for us to sit with God and pay attention. Whenever I have sat down to journal what He says or shows to me, or to practice paying attention to Him in some other way, I have been amazed. My heart is refreshed. The process reveals to me once again how beautiful He is, how much He loves me, and how much I love Him back. We were made to be with Him, to communicate with Him, to hear His voice. We *need* this.

One of my first experiments with learning to hear His voice helped me in several ways, specifically in growing my discernment to recognize when it was Him and when it was just my imagination.

Get a pen and a notebook, ask God to speak to you, and then write down what comes to you — everything you sense He *might* be telling you, even if it seems strange or "just you" at the time. When I do this simple exercise[2], I think, *That couldn't be God. And that couldn't be God.* But later, as I'm going over what I wrote, I can feel my spirit respond, and I realize, *That actually was God! And that was God, too.* One of the reasons this works is that our mind knows that by writing it down, we can evaluate it later, and so we stop evaluating in the moment, and this lets us listen better.

Jesus said that His sheep know His voice (John 10:4). This is a promise, a divine truth. The more we practice discerning His voice, the more our discernment grows and the more we'll be able to recognize when and what He is speaking to us.

THE STILL, SMALL VOICE

For a season, nearly everything God communicated to me happened internally (with my spiritual eyes) and not externally. God spoke to me through impressions, my emotions, and the mental pictures I mentioned previously.

Following that, I went through a time in which I was seeing more things with my physical eyes than I'd ever seen before. For instance, I would be sitting in my living room, and the cloud of God's glory would become so thick that I could barely see my wife, who was sitting just on the other end of the couch. Sometimes, I would see things come down and hover in front of me. They would

---

2 Virkler, *Dialogue with God*

give me enough time to focus on them, and then they would buzz off again.

Even though these things were extraordinary, I found that the more I paid attention to them, the more I ignored all the other things God was giving me, the things I wasn't seeing with my naked eye. After a while, not only did I stop seeing things internally, but I stopped seeing them with my physical eyes as well, because I was becoming dependent on my physical senses and not on faith.

As we begin seeing and hearing more clearly, it is very easy for us to begin to ignore the still, quiet voice — the whisper that encourages us to draw closer to God, to dwell on His secrets, the whisper that's not audible and often not even that clear.

The "greater" things are easier to accept than the still, quiet voice. It is good for us to expect and even ask for huge spiritual encounters, but we should never stop listening to the quiet, faint things that must be taken on faith. There are two reasons for their importance: One, they bring the glory of God because they require faith and dependency on Him; and two, nothing speaks intimacy more powerfully than a whisper.

THE REASON FOR THE WHISPER

Everything God does is birthed from love and His desire to be with His people. We won't be complete without this understanding.

The Bible describes our relationship with Him as being like that of a husband and wife. When we first try to picture this, we may think of the husbands and wives we sometimes see — the slightly burned out, slightly wounded spouses who may or may not be friendly toward one another. Many of them gave up long ago expressing what made them fall in love in the first place. Sometimes we expect God to be like this as well: slightly tired of us, a little bored, quick to correct our shortcomings, weary of our needs and questions and requests. However, the day we realize that God is still like a newlywed, our lives change forever.

What do newlyweds do? They never allow more than six inches between them. Anything greater than that feels like an inconceivable distance. They miss each other from across the room. They do a hundred little things that outsiders find sappy. They have to be near each other, and they feel like something is missing whenever distance temporarily separates them.

That is the reason for the whisper. When two people are only six inches apart, there is no need to shout. Speaking even at normal levels is often too intrusive. Instead, couples whisper, trying to draw as close as possible to one another, because of the great joy the other's nearness brings them.

I know we like the big presentations, the theophanies, the appearance of angels, the audible voice of God, the tangible manifestations of oil or gold on our hands — the power of God in us, the hot and the cold and the other stimuli. These are signs from God that we'd have to work really hard to ignore. However, they are not communications of intimacy.

God wants to clean out our ears, not in the areas of big revelation, but in this area of the whisper. The more I see with my physical eyes, the more I hear audibly, the more I have tastes and senses and manifestations, the more I realize how much I need the still, quiet voice. God's people are not fed by big revelation; we're fed by the whisper. Just as it is with everyday interactions, large presentations are usually for the benefit of others, for the group as a whole, but when someone is whispering, it is for one person only. It is intimate.

Intimacy is the still, quiet voice of God, the one that is so still and so quiet that it is easy to dismiss as not being anything more than our thoughts. Then, as we get good at hearing the whisper, God begins to whisper even more quietly — not to keep us distant but to draw us closer. He's becoming more intimate with us. He's teaching us how to be more still and more quiet in His presence, so we don't miss anything about Him — not a tone, not a reflection, not a posture. This is the level of intimacy God desires for us. He doesn't want His children to have to be distracted by visible signs; He wants us to be distracted by His whispers.

It can be difficult to get to that place of peace and quiet, especially for some of us. It can be very hard to sit with God for just five minutes, not with any prayer requests, not with anything we want, not with anything we're thinking, but just to sit before Him and pay attention to what He wants to communicate to us. That can be hard, but if we do this, if we even *attempt* to do it, He will come and fill us up, and the result will be that He uses us everywhere. We won't be able to avoid Him using us. Because we spent all that time looking *in* His eyes, when we look at others, we'll be looking *through* His eyes.

> **E**VERYTHING GOD DOES IS BIRTHED FROM LOVE AND HIS DESIRE TO BE WITH HIS PEOPLE.

We need to relearn how to be childlike and open. When

we spend time with Him, we don't have to "know" anything. In fact, in many cases, it's better if we don't, because then we don't have any preconceptions. We just want to spend time with Him, and we don't care what we're doing while we're doing it. Brother Lawrence, a monk living in the seventeenth century, would wash dishes with Jesus. Kings would come for his counsel, and he'd tell them to wait, because he was washing dishes with Jesus.[3]

I have been humbled by the quiet testimony of my children after they've spent time with the Lord. My daughter has come down from her room with a visible glow on her face after sitting with Jesus and talking with Him. She used to cry when she *didn't* see Jesus in her room. It would break her heart. What is a parent supposed to say after something like that? Some of us would tell her not to be concerned, because Jesus is with us all the time, even if we don't see Him. But I don't want to teach my children that it doesn't matter whether or not they see Jesus.

My daughter's faith shook my soul. The fundamental truth I've discovered through all this is that the days I spend with Jesus are better than the days I don't spend with Him. The more we know Jesus, the better and more fulfilling our entire lives will be.

ELIJAH
1 Kings 17–19

After a while, we begin to prefer the whisper to the shout, because when we hear God's whisper, we know He's putting something in us that we need.

---

3 Brother Lawrence, *The Practice of the Presence of God*

Elijah went through this at an intense level. At his word, it didn't rain for three years. He confronted the prophets of Baal and Asherah. He called down fire from Heaven that consumed not only the sacrifice but the soil and the entire water-soaked stone altar as well. All of this happened at his word — an act of faith that perhaps only Moses could understand.

When he had completed what God had given him to do, Elijah was utterly exhausted, and as we examine the story, he almost sounds clinically depressed. He had just experienced and participated in these incredible, mind-boggling acts of God, but now the pendulum was swinging. Instead of having great faith, he suddenly had great fear. He avoided everyone, deserted his apprentice, and told God, "I am the only one left." Overcome by his emotions, he became convinced that he wasn't going to survive and that he was completely alone.

> FINALLY, THERE CAME A STILL, SMALL VOICE. A WHISPER. AND THAT WAS WHERE GOD WAS.

In response, God sent him on a forty-day journey. He gave him angelic food twice to keep up his strength and then took him to the cave on Mount Horeb, where there was no food, no water, no distractions — where they could just talk.

You probably know the rest of the story. A wind came. It was so powerful that it "tore into the mountains and broke the rocks in pieces before the Lord." Then came an earthquake. Then a fire. But God was in none of these things. Finally, there came a still, small voice. A whisper. And that was where God was.

What many people miss is that the whisper was what Elijah

desperately needed. He *needed* God to speak to him in a still, quiet voice. After grandiose spiritual encounters have passed, after the crowds have gone home and the studio has been shut down for the night, the only thing left is our private intimacy with God. The more God does the "large" things, the more we spiritually, emotionally, and physically need Him not to do much in our presence. We just need Him to be with us.

If we can discern the still, quiet voice, we will rarely — if ever — find ourselves in situations in which we don't know what God is saying to us. We may not have a complete understanding of what He is doing or where He is leading us, but what we do have will be enough. He will fill our bones, calm our hearts, and feed our spirits. He will complete us. All with the whisper.

The whisper is directly related to God's peace. There is something about living in God's peace, with the whisper, that allows Him to come in and sustain our bodies. This, I believe, is why certain biblical leaders such as Enoch and Elijah lived until the time God literally removed them from the Earth. They knew Him, and it sustained them. Intimacy with the whisper is everything we need.

For some of us, learning to live in this peace will be the biggest fight we've had in a long time, but when we make proximity with God our home, the high places (great times with God) and the low places (when nothing seems to be going right) won't feel all that different. Surviving the low places won't be such a desperate affair anymore, because we understand that God still speaks to us in the low places, which makes all the difference in the world.

PROPHETIC & SEER Q&A:

QUESTION: The single reason I engage in the seers exercise is to hear more of Him, to see more of Him, and to understand more of Him. How do I recognize it's Him, and how do I recognize the enemy in the online exercises? I do not ask because I am afraid. God has shown me that He is always on guard for me and has sent prayer burdens from one country to another — incredible God we serve! I ask so I can learn to discern. So what do I need to know or ask — just call on God for discernment? Pray before it all? I want to be safe.

ANSWER: These are some relevant Scripture passages to consider:

> *"If anyone is willing to do His will, he will know of the teaching, whether it is of God or whether I speak from Myself."*
> — John 7:17

> *"So I say to you, ask, and it will be given to you; seek, and you will find; knock, and it will be opened to you. For everyone who asks receives, and he who seeks finds, and to him who knocks it will be opened. If a son asks for bread from any father among you, will he give him a stone? Or if he asks for a fish, will he give him a serpent instead of a fish? Or if he asks for an egg, will he offer him a scorpion? If you then,*

being evil, know how to give good gifts to your children, how much more will your heavenly Father give the Holy Spirit to those who ask Him!"
— Luke 11:9–13, NKJV

But solid food is for the mature, who because of practice have their senses trained to discern good and evil.
— Hebrews 5:14

The first passage lays down the principle that in order to know if something is God or not, you have to be willing to do His will. To the degree we are fully willing to do God's will is the degree we will know His will.

The second passage lays down the principle that if we seek God, we will find Him. So then, too, we will find as much of God as we are truly seeking for, and it will be as much purely Him as we truly want.

The third passage says that to discern good and evil takes practice. Our maturity in discernment is limited by our practice of it.

So in summation, to be truly solid in discerning God's revelation, we need to be fully submitted to His will (known and unknown), truly seeking and asking for only Him, and we need to keep practicing discernment until we are fully mature.

Every time we do not discern correctly, God will use it to instruct us and encourage us on in these three areas. So don't be afraid of making mistakes, because God will use them. Keep practicing so you have as many opportunities for growth as possible.

CHAPTER 5

RECEIVING REVELATION THROUGH OUR EMOTIONS

In an earlier chapter, I relayed the story of how my daughter and I saw my grandmother at her own funeral. At the time, I didn't understand why that would happen. She had been a believer, so I knew that she is with God and very much alive (John 11:25); I also knew that my seeing her wasn't necromancy (seeking to talk to the dead through demonic or soulish means) because God was the One showing her to me.[1] But why would I see her?

Eventually, I was able to ask this question of a man I considered a mentor.

"Well," he replied, "you saw her because she was there."

Okay, you're just messing with me now, I thought.

But the more I considered it, the more his answer began to make sense. Seers see and experience things because those things

---

1   For more information, see Appendix 3.

are there to be seen, and in many cases, those experiences are really happening. We may not see clearly or completely, and we may see a metaphoric representation of something — meaning, we're seeing it a certain way because God is highlighting a particular aspect of it. Perhaps the angel has a large nose because he has come to bring us discernment (the nose commonly represents discernment because we smell things to see if they are rotten or fresh), or perhaps the angel is carrying a calendar because he will help us to keep on schedule. Whether it seems to be literal or metaphoric, we're seeing it because it is there to be seen.

Once we acknowledge that what we're seeing is real, we're responding in faith, which produces more faith in us, strengthens our seer giftings, and opens us up to see and experience even more of God in the future. We are building a history with Him. Our *belief* in Him and His faithfulness is growing. We know He will speak to us, because He has proven that to us so often in the past.

In this chapter, we will be talking about our emotions and how the seer gifting affects them. Seers see what is actually there, but remember that *seeing* includes more than just spiritual sight. It includes all the senses: seeing, hearing, touching, smelling, and tasting, as well as any other way God communicates with us: impressions, thoughts, and instincts. It also includes our *emotions*.

We often receive revelation through what we feel or sense. Emotions tend to be highly sensitive, more so than our thoughts. This inherently sets them up to be affected by God's Spirit. However, it also sets them up to be sensitive to other sources as well. For example, there may be times when we get angry, frustrated, or depressed and assume we've done something to cause those emotions, but that may not be the case. It could be that the enemy is trying to oppress us in order to hinder the activity of God in our lives. There is also the possibility that what we're feeling may have very little to do with us at all. We could be picking up on what the people around us are feeling, their response to demonic attack, the enemy's plans, the enemy's actions, the demonic principalities over our region, God's plans, God's actions, trends in society, biochemical interactions going on in our bodies and even in others' bodies, positive and negative things happening in the world, etc. Because any of these could be influencing what we're feeling, we have to listen *through* our emotions, not necessarily *to* our emotions. They are a good barometer, but they are not always a good guide.

As it is with other forms of revelation, we need to take what we're feeling back to God, ask Him about it, wait for Him to confirm its meaning, and use discernment. I am convinced that of the three parts of our soul — mind, will, and emotions — our emotions are, by far, the most open to our spirit and therefore very sensitive to revelation from God. Listening to our hearts can lead to valid revelation. In fact, if we stop paying attention to our hearts, we'll find that our revelation as a whole begins to warp. Why? Because we're also not paying attention to the heart of God, the piece of Him that He's sharing with us. We're ignoring our consciences.

> ...WE NEED TO TAKE WHAT WE'RE FEELING BACK TO GOD, ASK HIM ABOUT IT, WAIT FOR HIM TO CONFIRM ITS MEANING, AND USE DISCERNMENT.

I ignored my emotions for years. A seasoned introvert, I

was severely repressed emotionally. Just after my wife and I met, she told me, "You know, Jim, I know your jokes and I know your intelligence, but I don't know how you feel about anything." I kept that part of me closed off.

So God tricked me. As I began to open myself to revelation from Him, almost all my initial impressions came through my emotions. I would have a strong emotional response for or toward other people that was completely unfounded; it felt like it was coming from me, but there was no reason for me to feel what I was feeling. I would feel happy, angry, bitter, passionate, or some other noticeable emotion, and I wouldn't know why. God opened my heart as I began to understand that I was feeling these things because I was picking up on His heart for someone else or what that person was struggling with.

For example, in the eighth grade, I had a crush on a girl who, in retrospect, I don't think I truly liked. I wasn't able to understand this at the time, but I saw what God was doing in her, and it drew my attention. The result was that I thought I liked her. However, along with being attracted to her, I had the strangest impression that she was being sexually abused at home. I didn't know a lot about sexual abuse; there wasn't much about it in the media those days. That strong reoccurring impression stuck with me for the next five years, and later, I learned that I had felt that way because God had given me a burden to intercede for her. He was showing me what was going on in her life so that I could pray about it.

Today, if I walk into a room and my attention is drawn to someone the way it was drawn to her, I know that God has something to show me about that person, either a word to give or something He wants me to carry before Him in prayer. He has trained me to ask, *Why do I feel this way? I have such passion for this person. I feel like weeping or crying or laughing. God, what are You saying about that?* I am then able to speak into the person's life. It took me fifteen years to understand and utilize this.

We need to learn to pay attention to what we're feeling, because that is often where revelation from God starts, and we could spend the rest of our lives receiving revelation for others this way. Learning to listen to God through our emotions is often the first credible form of revelation for beginning seers because it tends to happen so quickly. Yet it is not just a "low rung" on the prophetic scale. It can be very powerful.

Our emotions may be more sensitive than our thoughts, but they're often not as clear. In most cases, it will take deliberate practice on our part to discern the source of what's affecting us. Even if we don't fully understand right away, God will begin to teach us how to discern when something is coming from us, from someone else, from Him, or from the enemy. This is true of any sensory perception from the spiritual realm.

OVERCOMING FEAR OF THE SEER GIFTING

Because children are good at interacting with God, the enemy often targets us when we are young to shut down our giftings before we mature in them. He frequently does this through our emotions — namely, fear. As I help people grow in their seer giftings, I often hear stories of those who were harassed by the enemy as children. They would see horrible, frightening images in their rooms at night. They would hear voices, threats, inexplicable sounds, and other things that would terrify them. Many of them struggled with nightmares. The result was that some of these children came to believe their gifting was actually a curse, and some begged God to take it away altogether.

Each of us has a gifting and a calling, and the enemy wants to keep us from operating in them. If he can frighten us into forcibly ignoring or closing down our giftings, we won't be a threat to him.

As a child and later as a teenager, I spent years sleeping with a blanket over my head because I was afraid of what I would see. I grew up in a church that preached the Gospel, so I knew that demons couldn't harm me and that the angels were present to do only good, but I was so frightened that for twelve years, I cursed my eyes, praying that I wouldn't see anything. It wasn't until after I read Frank Peretti's *This Present Darkness*[2] that I felt comfortable facing the enemy. I stopped being afraid of him. I stopped being afraid of many things as I realized the authority God has given His children.

> GOD WILL BEGIN TO TEACH US HOW TO DISCERN WHEN SOMETHING IS COMING FROM US, FROM SOMEONE ELSE, FROM HIM, OR FROM THE ENEMY.

Many of us are in various stages of taking back what was shut down in us as children. Perhaps you experienced spiritual activity as a child and had non-rational thoughts that seemed more real than rational thoughts. Perhaps now you need to come before

---

2 Crossway Books, original printing 1986

God and repent for refusing the gifting He gave you. All giftings are from God. Satan can't give us any type of gifting, which is why he goes after people who have them. He is intent upon using those giftings for his own purposes or scaring us from using them at all.

After repentance, which restores us into right relationship with God, how do we begin to come out of this fear? The key to being unafraid of what we're experiencing *isn't* seeing only good things or knowing that our experiences are of God; the key is being unafraid either way — whether they're of God or of the enemy. This is important because it is difficult to discern anything accurately when we're afraid. We have to overcome our fear first, and then, as we do that, our discernment will increase. We'll be able to tell the source of what we're experiencing, and then we can get rid of what is from the enemy and welcome more of God.

As many of us have experienced, the moment of overcoming fear can be very, very hard. The only way I know how to make this mental transition is by becoming aggressive. If there is something in our house or bedroom at night, we want to know about it, so we can deal with it. That is a very intentional shift, and at the beginning, it can be difficult and frightening. But once we take that first step, it becomes easier.

Being afraid and running away is much more terrifying than facing our fears. If we determine to find out the source of what we're experiencing, no matter what that may be, our intentionality will diminish and then cut off our fear. Rampant fear comes not so much from being afraid as it does from running away, acting, or panicking in fear. Therefore, if we run *toward* what we're afraid of, the cycle will break, and we will find freedom. We will be able to use our giftings in peace. This process is similar to jumping out of an airplane. The thought of going out the door can scare some of us enough to keep us in our seats, but once we decide to do it, the intentionality of our decision causes the fear to lessen.

My son Caspian went through a season in which he was having nightmares almost every night. We prayed for him repeatedly. The nightmares would lessen, even leave for a time, but then they would return.

Finally, one morning, Caspian came downstairs and told me, "There was a witch in my bed last night."

"What did you do?" I asked.

"I killed her," he answered.

"Well, you know if that happens again, all you need to do is rebuke her in Jesus' name, and she will leave."

He gave me a funny look. "No, if it happens again, I'm going to kill her again!"

My young son is in the process of discovering the authority He has in God. Once he caught a glimpse of it, he realized that he didn't have to be tormented, and the repeated nightmares stopped.

God has given us authority over the enemy. It takes time to truly understand that, but as we begin to do so, the fear leaves, because we realize there isn't a reason for it.

If the enemy terrorized you as a child, you may have specific questions now concerning the usefulness, or even validity, of the seer gifting: *Why would I want to pursue this? How can you even suggest that this is a gifting from God?* Will studying your seer gifting cause you to begin to experience again what happened to

you as a child? Honestly, as we seek to restore the use of our giftings, there is the possibility that we will be opposed. We may see
some negative things. The enemy may try to frighten us and cause
us to feel helpless, as we did when we were young.

However, if we persist in keeping our eyes open and just
deal with the bad things as we see them, they will go away pretty
quickly. I know people who had horrific things happen to them in
childhood — not just spiritually but also emotionally and physically. When they started moving in the spiritual realm as adults,
they began to see some significantly bad things, but as they asked
God to remove those things and persisted in going forward, the
bad things went away. Their spiritual eyes were restored.

I can't promise you that you won't see demonic things, but
you can be prepared in faith to deal with them. Tell them to go in
the name of Jesus. Persist in doing that, because God promises
us that if we resist the devil, he will flee from us (James 4:7). The
reason you can resist him today but potentially couldn't when you
were a child is that you're now fully under your own authority.
When you were a child, you were in your parents' house and under
their authority. But you've grown into your own now, and if you
resist the enemy, he *will* flee from you. As you do this, God will restore your eyes, and He will restore the years. You'll begin to realize that He has been very prevalent in your life this entire time, but
because of what happened to you as a child, perhaps you couldn't
see it. Consequently, you'll come into a greater realization of your
purpose, and God will use you to help other people in ways that
will bring justice for what happened to you.

PROPHETIC & SEER Q&A:

QUESTION: I am wondering about the following: Doing the exercises, I realize we can also do them while in prayer for a person. Interceding, we can use the tools, but truth be said, I sometimes am scared to engage because I get so many pictures and visions it can overwhelm me with feelings for that person. Could it be that I am not to engage unless Jesus tells me to? Otherwise, I'd be in a rollercoaster of feelings all the time. Then how do I know when I should and when I shouldn't? Some of it is very encouraging, but it still scares me because of the unknown? Then after praying, I need to let go, which is hard because you feel for the person, and letting go into His hands is a must but not always easy. I have walked 18 years with Jesus but never like this. All of a sudden, I feel I need to put my mouth into action, kind of like you talk the talk, now walk the walk . . . and going out and doing stuff in faith is difficult to say the least. Is this all normal?

ANSWER: Yes, it is very normal for people who are aware of the spiritual realm to experience what you're experiencing. There is so much to see and hear and do that if we tried to pay attention to all of it, we'd never be able to move forward. We may even forget to breathe.

That is one of the reasons I like the Stir the Water exercises. They ask you to look for one thing and then ask six follow-up questions about the one thing you looked for. This gives you something to focus on.

Now, for some people, that is very helpful because they're not seeing anything. It's difficult for them to see, so the exercises help by telling them what to look for.

For people on the other end of the spectrum, such as yourself, the exercises can help them wade through the vast amounts of revelation they're receiving. "Out of all you *could* see, ask God about this one thing."

Regarding your specific question, when we go to pray for someone, and we receive so much information that we don't know where to start, the steps found in the exercises can help bring focus. Instead of being overwhelmed with *all* the potential revelation, we can look to see what Jesus is doing and then do it with Him. What is He saying about this person? What is He doing around him or her? How do we see Him ministering to this person? All we need to do is what He leads us to do.

Don't feel as if you have to see where Jesus is around the person *and* look for trees *and* look for spiritual clothing *and* do every spiritual exercise you've ever done. Just ask God to show you what to do in the moment. What He leads you to do may be different every single time; it may be similar several times in a row. But the key is to be guided by the Holy Spirit.

After we have done what God asked us to do, we should feel a release; the burden to pray should lift. Obviously, it isn't that we stop caring for the person, and it isn't that we couldn't do more, but we have done what God wanted us to do. That's usually the best time to stop. We won't easily become overwhelmed if we do only what He wants us to do.

It's like going to a nice restaurant and ordering something

off the menu. In most cases, we're going to order only one entree. That's it. Similarly, when we go to pray, there is a lot of different ways we could pray and a lot of revelation we could get. But instead of being weighed down by all the possibilities, we just need to ask God, "How should I do this?" He will lead us. We should "order" one thing, and then enjoy it.

As we serve God, there is always a lot we *could* do for Him. We could become missionaries, study music, write worship songs, write books, spread the Gospel by going door to door in our neighborhood — we could be busy all the time. But we don't have to worry about all the things we *could* do. All we need to do is the one thing He's leading us to do in the moment. This gives us room to enjoy that activity with Him, without feeling like we have an unending to-do list. And when we're done, we're done.

If we have a history of knowing that we've done what God has given us to do, we won't feel guilty because we didn't do more. We won't feel inadequate because we didn't do everything we could have done. Instead, we'll understand that we did what He wanted, and that was all we needed to do.

CHAPTER 6

HOW DO I
STOP IGNORING GOD?

Americans often go through an auditory "culture shock" when spending time in an underdeveloped area of the world. If we're used to constant sound but then move to the middle of nowhere, where there is no electricity, no electric or gas motors, no lights, no highways, no cars — all of a sudden, the noise that normally pervades us every day and every moment is gone. At first, we may not be bothered by its absence, but after a while, it starts to unnerve us because we sense that something is missing, and we usually can't tell what it is. We learn at an early age to automatically filter out all the extra sound. It is not possible for us to pay attention to all of it, all the time. But when it is gone, we notice.

This is in the natural. In the supernatural, we are constantly bombarded by spiritual "noise" as well. Not all of it is of God; as we discussed in Chapter Five, we can pick up on a variety of different senses and feelings that are coming from other sources. Some seers can't even walk through a grocery store without seeing, hearing, feeling, and sensing a host of different things, from a host of different sources. There is *a lot* happening all around us, almost all the time, which is rather peculiar when viewed in a certain light, because many Christians feel as if they're not very good at hearing from God. They don't feel close to Him, and they don't know how to begin to communicate with Him on a daily basis. Hopefully, as you go through this book, that will change. His invitation is for each of us:

> *Come and see the works of God,*
> *Who is awesome in His deeds toward the sons of men.*
> — Psalm 66:5

We have such a history of redemption — Noah, Moses, Jesus — and every time God delivered His people, the point was to bring us back to the place where He could walk with us and speak with us.

Communication is one of the utmost desires of God's heart. I'm astounded by how much, how often, and how eagerly He speaks to us. The spiritual atmosphere around us is moving — things are happening, being brought forth, being revealed. Our spirits pick up on all God is communicating to us, even if our minds are not aware of it. They hear what He is saying to us about our thought processes;

> COMMUNICATION IS ONE OF THE UTMOST DESIRES OF GOD'S HEART.

our painful childhood experiences; opportunities for growth; what He wants us to pray for; what He tried to tell us yesterday that we missed; what He has to tell us about our future; what He wants us to know about His absolute, complete delight with us, all the time, every day; what He wants us to see; all the angelic activity around us; and so much more. We are surrounded by this constantly.

When I take the time to pause and look into the spiritual realm, there is so much to see that I have to momentarily withdraw, take a deep breath, start over, and ask God to show me the *one thing* He wants me to see. If I don't do that, my prayer will become, "God, I'm sorry, but there's too much. My brain is fried. I can't listen. I can't even look right now."

If we look, we *will* see. We'll see spiritual elements on people; we'll see angels and strange creatures, fruit trees growing in different places, unordinary elements in unexpected locations, and so much more. We'll see Jesus over here touching this person and that person. We'll see Him touching us. We'll see extraordinary things that we would never see in the physical realm, but they are completely natural and normal in the realm that is eternal.

With all of this happening all the time, how is it possible that we often aren't aware of it? In this chapter, we're going to talk about the four stages of ignoring God and how to recognize them in our lives.

DISMISSING WHAT DOESN'T MAKE SENSE

We touched on this first stage in previous chapters: dismissing what doesn't make sense. To different degrees, all of us have learned to block out what our spirits are sensing and to pay attention to what seems logical in our human reasoning. This is not always negative, but a strict adherence to it has resulted in generation after generation of Christians who believe that if something doesn't follow earthly, cultural rules of analytical thinking, it doesn't exist.

Again, picking and choosing what is important enough to focus on isn't always harmful; however, it is a problem when we pick and choose with the Holy Spirit and the unexplainable things He may be showing us. By definition, revelation *reveals* something. We didn't know it beforehand, and we can't comprehend it until Someone explains it to us. Dismissing what doesn't make sense is the first stage of ignoring God.

IGNORING OR HIDING FROM WHAT WE DON'T WANT TO HEAR

If you are married, have honest friends, or spend a lot of time with your parents, you are probably more than familiar with the concept of "constructive criticism." People give us advice, and what they're saying may be a good or even necessary idea, but we don't always want to think about it. In that moment, we are not willing to change, and so we dismiss what they say.

I used to work for a man named Greg Mapes, and he has never suggested anything that I didn't come to appreciate or wish that I had done after the fact. He usually doesn't come out and *tell* me to do something; instead, he presents his advice with options. "Jim," he'll say, "you may want to think about doing this." I then have the opportunity to shrug it off or go ahead and do it.

Everything he suggests typically has a cost involved; it could be monetarily expensive, or it could be something I simply don't want to consider.

In a similar way, not everything the Holy Spirit shows us will be simple to process mentally or easy to accomplish. Often, He may present us with something that we know would be a good step to take, but it comes with a price. Perhaps the topic is too painful for us, or it could be beyond our current paradigm:

That just couldn't be God. He wouldn't ask me to do that.

I just can't do that. I have too many things on my plate today.

That is far too grandiose for somebody like me. He may feel that way about somebody who's perfect, but He wouldn't ever say that about somebody like me.

The cost is higher than we're willing to pay, and so we choose to ignore it or pretend it isn't relevant. This is the second stage of ignoring God.

MODIFYING WHAT WE CLEARLY UNDERSTOOD THE FIRST TIME

All of these stages are serious, but the third stage is the first that is inherently dangerous. It usually occurs between someone who is in authority and someone who is under that authority — parent and child, employer and employee, etc. We know what we are supposed to do. We heard and understood the order the first time, but we don't want to do it, and so we *change* the order to mean something other than what we originally knew it meant.

This stage corrupts the integrity of our inner spiritual ear. In the Garden, Adam and Eve knew what God had told them, but then Satan came along and asked, "What did God *really* say?"

God hadn't implied anything to them. He had been very clear: "You may eat from every tree in the Garden except this tree — the Tree of the Knowledge of Good and Evil. If you eat of this tree, you will die." The order couldn't have been any clearer than that.

But Satan skewed their thinking. "Did He *really* say that? Did He really mean that? Is that really true?"

As humans, something within us is very willing to modify or downplay what people in authority, including God, tell us to do. We hold on to just enough of the original order or statement that we believe we are still within the proper boundaries, that we're doing what we have been told to do. We don't change the entire meaning — just the part we don't like. For example, when we tell our children to pick up their bedroom, that order pertains to the entire room, not just the bed or the floor. But often, when we return to check on their progress, the room hasn't been cleaned; everything that was on the floor is now on the bed or vice versa. They might argue that they "picked up" the room, but clearly, they didn't follow the order.

> AS HUMANS, SOMETHING WITHIN US IS VERY WILLING TO MODIFY OR DOWNPLAY WHAT PEOPLE IN AUTHORITY, INCLUDING GOD, TELL US TO DO.

Unfortunately, this stage does not pertain to children only. It becomes more dangerous as we mature, because as our capacity for wisdom grows, so does our capacity for cunning. Often, we aren't trying to be cunning or deceitful; we're just doing what *we* think is best.

I used to work in Manhattan as a computer programmer. Our project manager knew nothing about programming. In our weekly meetings, he would tell us what to do, and then he would leave. All of us knew that he didn't know what he was doing, so after he left, we would sit there and figure out who knew how to do what he wanted. We would then redistribute the work he had given us. If we didn't do that, he would be fired, because as a group, we wouldn't be able to complete what his bosses had given him to do. But we also discovered that there was a real tendency for us to go ahead and do what we wanted anyway, usurping his authority. We would modify the directions we'd been given, which is the third stage of ignoring God.

OPPOSING WHAT WE DON'T WANT TO HAPPEN

This fourth stage is the full-blown version of ignoring God. At this stage, when we realize God is about to do something that opposes our wishes, we attempt to keep it from happening. We work to ensure that the opposite will happen instead, which means we are actively engaging Him as our enemy.

It is as serious as it sounds. Many of us think in surprise, *Engaging God as my enemy? I would never do that! Surely only "bad" people would do something like that.* But this trap is easy to fall into. Let's look at a few biblical examples.

KING HEROD
Mark 6, Luke 23

Herod had a love-hate relationship with John the Baptist. John voiced powerful, intriguing ideas, and because Herod had Jewish roots, he was somewhat interested in hearing what the man had to say. However, John was offending him, and, worse than that, he was offending the queen. Most of us know the story. Eventually, Herod was tricked by his wife and her daughter and had John killed.

Some time after that, when Jesus was arrested and taken into custody, Pilate didn't want to be involved, so he sent Him to Herod. What did Jesus say to Herod?

Absolutely nothing.

Herod had brought himself to the point where he was the enemy of what God was doing, and God wasn't going to tell him anything.

This fourth stage of ignoring God is the spiritual equivalent of puncturing our eardrums. Once we are at this stage, the only thing that will rescue us is repentance. Repentance is necessary in all four stages, but this stage involves a significant amount of self-deception, which blinds us. In other words, when we set ourselves up to oppose God, we often don't realize it is God we are opposing. If we did, we would probably stop.

This was what Gamaliel cautioned the other Pharisees about when they were having issues with the Apostles (Acts 5:33–39, emphasis mine): "Let's be careful. Let's not kill these men, because if we do, we might *find ourselves* opposing God."

KING SAUL
1 Samuel 9–24

Saul is probably the best biblical example of someone whose walk started well but then grew sour. He went through all four stages of ignoring God.

A short time before he became the first king of Israel, his father's donkeys wandered away, and Saul was told to go out and find them. While he and his servant were on their search, they ran out of money and were about to run out of food. They didn't know what else to do, so the servant suggested they pay Samuel the Seer a visit.

When they arrived, Samuel essentially told them, "Don't worry about the lost donkeys. They've been found, and now everyone's worried about you — but aren't you the man all Israel is looking for?" He then said that Saul was going to be the first king of Israel.

This revelation was completely out of Saul's realm of thinking. We know this because of the way he responded: "What? Don't you know who I am? I'm a Benjamite — from the smallest tribe in all Israel. And my family is the least of all the families of Benjamin. Why in the world did you say that to me? Samuel, I know you're a great man and none of your words fall to the ground, but you're speaking gibberish to me right now." This is the first stage of ignoring God; Saul dismissed what he didn't understand.

After that, he quickly moved into the second stage. In 1 Samuel 10, Saul's uncle asked him, "Where have you been?"

Saul told him all that had happened — except for one little thing. He left out the part about becoming king. In his insecurity, he couldn't accept the possibility, and so he ignored it.

The hiding phase followed. When Samuel summoned the nation to choose their king, Saul realized what was coming next, so he went and hid behind the baggage. He didn't want to deal with the thing he feared. Even though the Bible calls him "a choice and handsome son," a man who was a head taller than everyone else, he had very little self-confidence. I believe that the possibility of rejection by the people was too great a risk for him.

The modifying stage followed. After Saul had been crowned, Samuel specifically told him, "Wait seven days for me to bring an offering."

So Saul waited. He wasn't an evil man; he had good intentions. But then the testing came. Samuel didn't arrive when he said he would, and Saul suddenly found himself once again facing the core issue that crippled him: rejection. His army began scattering, and in an effort to maintain control, he went ahead and offered the sacrifice.

Samuel arrived just as the sacrifice had ended. He asked Saul, "What have you done?"

Relying on human wisdom, Saul had done what he thought was best. As of yet, he didn't realize how bad a move that had been. "The men were getting restless, the Philistines were coming to attack me, and I hadn't sought God's favor. I knew I had to do this."

He found an excuse — some reason for him to proceed according to his desire — and modified what he had been told to do. In his own mind, he had more or less done what God had asked of him.

The key here is that Saul did what *he thought* was best. Granted, God gives each of us wisdom, and common sense is often the Holy Spirit leading us, but Saul modified his orders; he did what he originally knew he was not supposed to do.

Again, this pit is not difficult for well-meaning children of God to find. For example, I have four very active boys, and I will tell one of them, "Don't hit your brother."

He will go ahead and punch him anyway.

"Why did you do that when I told you not to?" I ask.

"He hit me first!"

They know the rules, but they modify them because the excuse is more in line with their desire or logic.

A second common modification is for reasons of self-preservation: We modify what God has said so that we, or those we care for, will be safe.

There have been times when God has clearly told me, "Prefer your wife."

"Okay, God. I'll prefer my wife." And I will, until there is an issue that comes up and I start reasoning it out. *I would love to prefer my wife in this, but we're talking about two hundred dollars here. It is safer for us financially to do what I want to do, so I'll prefer her next time. I'm sure God will understand.*

We have a seemingly valid reason not to do what God said, so we modify the order.

Saul modified the instructions twice. In the second situation, Samuel had told him, "God intends to punish the Amalekites for how they treated His people when they came up out of Egypt. Kill every one of them, including the king, and destroy everything they own. Leave nothing that belongs to them."

He said to "kill all of them." That is hardly open to interpretation. But again, Saul did what he thought was best instead of doing what God had plainly told him to do. He destroyed all the men, but he took the king alive and allowed his men to keep the best animals. Why did he spare the animals? As he explained to Samuel later, "We wanted to give the Lord an offering." It sounds like good reasoning, perhaps even wisdom, but it wasn't.

There is a spirit behind this third stage of ignoring God. Modification is not actually about what we do or don't do; it is an issue of the heart.

Jesus told His followers in John 14:15, "'If you love Me, you will keep My commands.'" There is a clear, significant relationship between intimacy with God and doing what He has told us to do.

"I am grieved that I made Saul king," the Lord told Samuel. "He has turned away from Me."

Saul then came to the last stage of ignoring God, which is opposing His will. Samuel told Saul what God had said: Because Saul hadn't done as God instructed, God had rejected him as king. Saul's worst fear rushed in upon him. He was being rejected, this time by God Himself. It was too much for him, and he broke. He grabbed Samuel with such force that he ripped Samuel's clothes. He begged him to stay so that he wouldn't look stupid in front of his men.

But Samuel told him, "God is going to rip the kingdom away from you and give it to your neighbor."

Saul then knew he was destined to lose the thing he hadn't wanted in the first place, but instead of turning back to God and seeking His favor, he braced himself for the storm. Later, when David killed Goliath and drew the public eye away from Saul, Saul probably began to worry, *This is the man God selected to replace me.* But even then, he did not acknowledge it as God. Instead, he attributed it to man. *David is going to try to take my kingdom away from me!* he thought. *I must control the situation so I can keep my position safe.*

He did what Gamaliel told the Pharisees not to do: Somewhat unintentionally, he put himself in the position of opposing God. He cut off his own spiritual leadership and sank so far that the little wisdom he did have became even less, and he started making some very irrational decisions. He attacked David. He attacked his own people. He even attacked his son. Paranoia crept in, and God allowed a demonic spirit to plague him. He became truly delusional.

All of us possess this same innate desire to protect ourselves. Having that desire isn't sin, but the importance we place on it can lead us into sin. God is our Protector — we are not. Therefore, if our focus in life is the protection of our comfort zones and insecurities, we will end up avoiding everything that would potentially threaten them: this means whoever and whatever disagrees with us, jeopardizes our pride, pricks our insecurities, or makes us feel as if we're not in control. And God

> MODIFICATION IS NOT ACTUALLY ABOUT WHAT WE DO OR DON'T DO; IT IS AN ISSUE OF THE HEART.

would potentially do all of those things. When He begins to set in order something we fear, many of us instinctively try to keep it from happening. We don't realize we're resisting Him; we wouldn't put it in those words. But that is often what occurs. Sometimes, the things we've spent our entire lives trying to stop are the very things God created us for. The Apostle Paul is a good example of this. He spent years persecuting Christians, only to become one of the most influential Christians of all time.

Once we've begun resisting God like this, the only thing that can bring us to repentance is a true encounter with Him, because it has become a matter of self-deception. Non-Christians aren't concerned with doing God's will. Why would they be? But as Christians, we know we're supposed to be righteous, listen to God, respond to Him, and obey Him. Very few Christians who are actively seeking God don't believe these things. So when we have internally decided that our own desires are more important than God's, we have to trick ourselves into believing that we're really not opposing Him, that we're actually doing what He wants us to do.

Self-deception often allows religion and self-righteousness to creep in; we think our actions are right and appropriate and don't allow discernment to tell us otherwise. When I was fourteen years old, a new pastor took over the conservative evangelical church my family attended, and some of the things he tried to introduce caused turmoil in the congregation. In retrospect, I can recognize that the Spirit of God was moving and inviting people into a deeper relationship with Him, but most of us didn't see that at the time. Even though I was young, I was aware of the tension.

What was the main issue behind this disturbance? Whether or not people should raise their hands in worship.

Now that I'm on the other side of that, all the turmoil caused by this simple idea seems almost humorous, but when you're in the midst of such unknown territory, it appears very serious. At the time, I wondered, *If I raise my hand, how do I know if it's God or if it's me? Because if I raise my hand and it is me, that would be bad. I don't know what would happen, but I know it would be very bad.*

I can remember certain church members going out of their way to make sure that others weren't "given to the flesh" in worship. Their reasoning was that they didn't want the flesh ruling in the church, which doesn't sound like a negative desire. It even sounds wise, but now that times have changed, most of us would probably agree that in the grand scheme of life, the church could have directed all that effort and energy toward more important matters.

Submission to God allows Him to come in and change our thought processes, focuses, and what we consider to be important. Submission to Him is what keeps us from falling into the same trap that snared Saul and Herod and countless others through history. Submission, however, is not something we stumble across at random. Like discernment, it takes practice, perseverance, and an intimate relationship with God.

MARY
Luke 1–2

Though they are easy traps to fall into, it is possible to avoid all four stages of ignoring God. A young teenage girl managed to do so at the beginning of the New Testament. She was told by an angel that she was going to have a baby.

That would be difficult revelation to hear. *I'm a virgin, and I'm pregnant — with the Son of God.* If I were Mary, it would be difficult for me not to automatically reply, "Gabriel, it's great that you came and told me this, but I'll believe it when you go and send God, because I'm gonna need some more confirmation."

But she took the high road. She started off a little hesitant: "How will this be? For I don't know a man. It's not physically possible." Her final response, however, showed her heart: "Let it be to me as You have said." I can imagine her thinking, *This doesn't make any sense, God. This is gibberish to me. I don't understand, but let it be as You have said. I will hold on to this.*

Not only did she embrace what God told her, but she sought to strengthen her faith in the word as well. Gabriel had told her that her cousin Elizabeth was now expecting, too, and so Mary went to spend time with her. This reaction is a little different than hiding behind the baggage, and we see Mary continually responding this way. When Jesus stayed behind in Jerusalem and was missing for three days, she panicked, as any parent would. When she and her husband finally found Him, she basically told Him, "Don't You ever do this to me again!"

> NOT ONLY DID SHE EMBRACE what GOD TOLD HER, BUT SHE SOUGHT TO STRENGTHEN HER FAITH IN THE WORD AS WELL.

He answered, "Why were you worried? Didn't you know I'd be in My Father's house?"

The Bible says she treasured these things in her heart. She held on to and meditated on the things she didn't understand.

Why was that important? Because these things weren't going to make any sense until Jesus was thirty-three years old and dead and risen again.

Most of the things Mary heard from Anna and Simeon (Luke 2:25–38) and the other things she experienced weren't going to be understood for thirty years, but she treasured them in her heart — stuff that seemed like "nonsense" and gibberish. Yet in the end, her questions were answered.

In conclusion, the most important thing we could ever do as seers is seek God — without a set of rules or boundaries, just seek Him and get to know Him as He is. When we are open to His Holy Spirit, we are open to His leading, and He can come to us and say, "I know the plans I have for you. You may not be able to picture them now. They will be too great for your mind to comprehend, but I am with you, and I can make them happen."

Prophetic & Seer Q&A:

QUESTION: What do we do when all we see is for other people and never ourselves? It is great to be able to bless other people, but I also want to see for me, too. I think I would feel much less "lost" if I saw for me now and again. And, if we are only ever seeing for other people, what might the reason for that be?

ANSWER: One of the seer gifting's primary uses is to see for other people. This usually happens first and tends to happen most frequently.

It is rare for people to never see anything for themselves, but it's not unheard of. The best solution for this is to be around others, where you're seeing for them and they're seeing for you.

God may allow such a condition to persist so that you develop a need for other people. I'm not saying that God *caused* this to happen so that you'd be forced to let others see for you, but He's probably not releasing you to see for yourself until you have a sense of community. If you consistently see for others *and* for yourself, then others might need you, but you wouldn't need them. However, if you're seeing for others and they're seeing for you, then you need one another. As you grow in interdependency, this condition will probably lift.

It is often much simpler for us to have faith for other people than for ourselves. Why? Because it is easier for us to believe good things for others and have hope for them than it is for us to believe positive things about ourselves. We have opinions and beliefs about ourselves that may be in the way of what He wants to tell us, so we typically are more open and objective about what God says concerning us when the words are coming through other people.

It could be that God is telling us wonderful things about us and for us, but we don't have the faith or hope to believe them. As others see them for us, we'll gradually become more open to seeing them, too.

Again, the solution is the same: Be around other people, so they can see for you and you can see for them. Grow as a community, and then, if there are any issues within you, they will naturally begin to alleviate. For instance, if you don't believe the truth about yourself or don't have hope for your own life, the fact that other people do will impart that to you, and you'll start being able to see more for yourself.

CHAPTER 7

INTERACTING WITH THE SUPERNATURAL

Some years ago, I was attending a Bible study at my pastor's house. When I walked into the living room, I immediately saw a tree growing out of the floor. Reddish-orange fruit was hanging on the branches.

I knew that depending on the context, red can mean anointing and orange can mean perseverance, so I discerned that if I ate the fruit, God would anoint me to encourage the persistence of the people present. They could have heard from God for themselves about this, but I needed to do it for them because they most likely didn't see the tree.

In order for me to follow God's leading in this instance, I would need to participate in what was going on, to cooperate with what I was perceiving. He was inviting me to interact with the spiritual realm.

Usually when I interact with the spiritual realm, I do so in the spirit — that is, if other people were watching, they wouldn't be able to see me doing anything out of the ordinary. But this specific time, I felt that I should actually *do* what God had put on my heart to do. So during the meeting, as nonchalantly as possible, I reached up and ate the fruit off the tree, trying to make it look like I was simply involved with worship.

As this fruit went into my spirit, God began to give me revelation, and later during the ministry time, I was able to give people powerful words. There were individuals in the group that night who had never been there before, and they asked, "How did you know that?"

"God speaks," I told them. "He gave me a very simple understanding."

I ate the fruit off the tree, discerned by faith what the fruit represented, and then spoke those things into the people. Even though they may not have seen the tree, they still received its fruit. The outcome was essentially the same.

That evening after everyone left, the pastor asked me, "How did you get those words?"

I could imagine what he was thinking: *You had an impression of something, and you went with it. It ended up being right, and so you received more.*

But that wasn't how it happened, not exactly, and I knew God wanted me to give him the details. So I told him what had happened.

Afterward, he looked at me blankly. "Wow. That's really good you didn't share that with anybody."

"You live in Narnia," his wife told me, referencing C.S. Lewis' classic children's series.

Why would God show me a fruit tree growing in my pastor's living room? Why would He want me to interact with it the way I had? Whenever God communicates with us, He says what He says the way He says it because He is showing us who He is. He is revealing Himself to us. It is an invitation to press into Him and seek Him out and know Him better. That evening at my pastor's house, He revealed Himself as a tree, one that bore fruit — His promises — for certain people present. I learned more about Him and my seer gifting through that experience.

He could always use words to communicate with us, but depending on the circumstances, words may not be the best representation of who He is. Every time He gives us the opportunity to interact with good, godly things in the spiritual realm, He is whispering, *Come. Touch this. Do this, and you will see Me as I am. Get to know Me better.*

As always, discernment is necessary. When we become aware of something in the spiritual realm, the first thing we should do is ascertain its source. We may know the nature of it right away, or it may take a few minutes of waiting on God for the quiet "spark" of His confirmation. If our discernment (or even what we *think* is our discernment) tells us that what we're seeing is something dark, it is probably something dark. We should still seek God about what we should do with it, but we shouldn't volunteer to interact with

> WHENEVER GOD COMMUNICATES WITH US, HE SAYS WHAT HE SAYS THE WAY HE SAYS IT BECAUSE HE IS SHOWING US WHO HE IS.

it, because we don't want to connect with something that isn't of God, nor do we want to take any steps beyond what He intended.

Whether it is something of God or not, there may be times when He doesn't want us to do anything with what we're seeing; He may want us only to be aware of its presence. It could be to train us in our gifting. If it is something dark, He may want us to rebuke it or caution others about its presence. But no matter what it is, we should always pray about it and seek Him about it. As we practice our discernment in this area, we will learn to recognize when He wants us to be still and when He wants us to step forward.

Interacting with the spiritual realm is a very biblical principle. The Bible contains the stories of several people who saw what God was showing them and then interacted with what they were seeing. In this chapter, we will talk about their experiences and go over what it can mean to "interact" with Heaven.

EZEKIEL
Ezekiel 3–4, 8

In my opinion, Ezekiel is one of the strangest books in the Bible. Even the man's name was strange. He looked into the spiritual realm, recorded what he saw, shared it with others, and has since become known as the weird-named guy who wrote the weird book.

If he had shared his understanding but kept to himself the way he'd received it, he wouldn't be viewed today as one of the strange prophet-seers of the Bible; he probably would be known as a profound teacher. Perhaps people would even consider him down-to-earth. Instead, he did what God asked him to do and gave us a glimpse of what it can look like to interact with the spiritual realm. He didn't just observe it; he became a part of what was going on and recorded his experiences.

Like the spiritual realm itself, interacting with the spiritual realm doesn't follow a set pattern; it can look like several different things. For example, I went through a season in which I would ask God every morning, "Are there any spiritual beings around me?" Often I would see an angel. I would see patterns in the wings and feathers, a blue or purple sash, some type of plaid kilt, etc., but sometimes the angel would be holding a platter, and on the platter would be something important. At times it was a vial of oil, and when I took that oil and poured it on my head, I would be overcome by the presence of God. I would feel Him so intimately and strongly. On other occasions, I would see the angel carrying a large pair of eyeglasses, and God would tell me, "This is to correct your vision." I would "put them on" in faith and discover that I could see more clearly into the spiritual realm, or

> LIKE THE SPIRITUAL REALM ITSELF, INTERACTING WITH THE SPIRITUAL REALM DOESN'T FOLLOW A SET PATTERN; IT CAN LOOK LIKE SEVERAL DIFFERENT THINGS.

that I hadn't been seeing as clearly as I'd thought in certain areas. Because I looked, I saw, but because I interacted with what I saw, I received.

When we interact with what we see, it affects us. Depending on the circumstances, it can cause us to experience change at a great level. Ezekiel was affected constantly, sometimes in very dramatic ways. For instance, at one point, he was caught up by his hair and floated over the elders (chapter 8). Another time, he received food through what he was seeing:

> *Then He said to me, "Son of man, eat what you find;*
> *eat this scroll, and go, speak to the house of Israel."*
>
> *So I opened my mouth, and He fed me this scroll.*
>
> *He said to me, "Son of man, feed your stomach and*
> *fill your body with this scroll which I am giving you."*
> *Then I ate it, and it was sweet as honey in my mouth.*
>
> *Then He said to me, "Son of man, go to the house of*
> *Israel and speak with My words to them."*
> — Ezekiel 3:1–4

When we read this passage, we can see that there is a very clear connection between Ezekiel's interaction with what he was seeing and God's giving him words to speak to Israel. By following God's leading to participate in what he was seeing, his experience became larger and more profound.

ISAIAH
Isaiah 6

Isaiah also interacted with what he saw. When God opened his eyes and showed him the Throne Room, it terrified him. He realized how sinful he was and sought to change:

So I said:

"Woe is me, for I am undone!
Because I am a man of unclean lips,
And I dwell in the midst of a people of unclean lips;
For my eyes have seen the King,
The LORD of hosts."

Then one of the seraphim flew to me, having in his
hand a live coal which he had taken with the tongs
from the altar. And he touched my mouth with it,
and said:

"Behold, this has touched your lips;
Your iniquity is taken away,
And your sin purged."

Also I heard the voice of the Lord, saying:

"Whom shall I send,
And who will go for Us?"

Then I said, "Here am I! Send me."
— Isaiah 6:5–8, NKJV

What Isaiah saw caused him to realize the state of his soul. He
engaged in what God was doing — he didn't simply observe it,
but he responded to it and was changed by it. Then, because the

change occurred, he was able to hear God's request and volunteer for assignment. We don't see that he was able to do that beforehand.

When we interact with what we see — this may mean praying about it — it affects us. Seeing is only the first step. If we stop there, the experience may accomplish only part of what God intended.

When we interact with what we see, God may equip and empower us. He may release anointing, words, revelation, purpose, and destiny. He often breaks off strongholds and removes the blinders that keep us from knowing Him and His heart for us. Interacting with the spiritual realm can be life changing and destiny inducing.

DANIEL
Daniel 2, 5, 6

A contemporary of Ezekiel, Daniel had many bizarre experiences as well, but in addition, he had something that Ezekiel did not seem to have: favor. Throughout Daniel's career as a prophet-seer, his revelation brought him favor with kings.

When Nebuchadnezzar threatened his wise men with death if they didn't both interpret his dream *and* tell him what he had dreamed, Daniel went to him and said, "Wait until tomorrow, and then I'll be able to do what you ask." God gave him the revelation; Daniel reported to the king, and the king promoted him.

Later, Daniel interpreted writing on the wall for King Belshazzar and was promoted again. He was advanced yet again after jealous men had him sealed in a den filled with ravenous lions. That time, not only was Daniel promoted, but King Darius fed Daniel's enemies to the lions in his place, along with their entire families.

God cleared the way before and after Daniel because the man used his authority in accordance with God's will. He had wisdom in handling revelation. Ezekiel also had wisdom, but not once do we see him being promoted based on the revelation he received. Instead, he was told that God was sending him to a people hard-headed and hard-hearted who wouldn't listen to him.

> WE NEED TO BE MORE CONCERNED WITH WHAT GOD IS DOING THAN WITH WHAT SEEMS TO BE SUCCESSFUL ACCORDING TO HUMAN WISDOM.

This introduces an important point to understand. The revelation Daniel received saved people's lives, but we don't see any national change for Israel based on what Ezekiel saw and heard. His was a walk of blind faith: God saw him as successful, but from an outsider's perspective, the opposite most likely seemed more accurate.

This principle is vital for all of us to understand, no matter our gifting. God has specific purposes for our giftings and talents, and we need to be submitted to Him even in times of confusion, when we don't understand what He is doing. Both Daniel and Ezekiel interacted with the spiritual realm. They each participated in what God was doing, but what He was doing was very different with each of them. This meant that their apparent success — what the world saw — was very different as well.

We need to be more concerned with what God is doing

than with what seems to be successful according to human wisdom. This is a sign of maturity. Some seers are called to speak to heads of government, and some of us are called to speak to our neighbors and friends. In the world's eyes, one of those may seem more important than the other, but it isn't. They are both the same. Through his interactions with the spiritual realm, Daniel saw great change in the lives of the people. Ezekiel did not, yet that did not mean he was on a lower rung than his contemporary.

We may go through seasons in which we see God move in incredible ways as a result of our prayers and other interactions with the spiritual realm. Then we may go through seasons in which it feels as if we're barely hanging on, and there doesn't seem to be any change anywhere. But if we do what we are called to do, God considers us successful, no matter the outcome or how insignificant our actions may seem at the time.

PROPHETIC & SEER Q&A:

QUESTION: I have heard a lot of people talk about seeing lights and even photographing them, but they don't know what they are about. Can you help?

ANSWER: From a physics standpoint, whenever someone sees or photographs lights, points of light, or circles of light, we know that there is something emitting energy right there. It could be any number of things: good, bad, of a physical origin, of an angelic or demonic origin; it could be the human spirit or the Holy Spirit. If we want to know what's happening around us, we first need to know the source of what we're seeing.

With photographs in particular, it can be difficult to tell the source, because the camera has no discernment. We could go to a rave and take a picture that has a ton of really cool, bright-white orbs in it. Then we could go to a church service and get a picture that has just as many orbs or one that has none. The camera isn't going to tell us the source of what we're seeing. In order to know the source, we need to have discernment, preferably in the moment.

Physical cues (such as lights and orbs) provoke us to wonder what's going on. We need to take what we're seeing or sensing and go back to the Holy Spirit for discernment and understanding. He may tell us right away; we could know what we're seeing the moment we see it, but sometimes even if the information comes so immediately that it feels like "just us," it could be originating with

Him. It shouldn't be coming from a physical trick, deducement, or even human wisdom. It should be coming from discernment. We never get away from the need to grow in discernment. Hebrews tells us that discernment comes by reason of use, so the more we practice it, the more we grow in it.

My concern with people taking pictures of orbs and lights, or even seeing things with their physical eyes, is that they may start relying on *sight* rather than faith, discernment, wisdom, and the Holy Spirit. The more we rely on sight rather than faith, the more likely it is that we will have a crisis of faith when something changes on us. For instance, cameras change; the designers could write software that removes all the lights and circles from our pictures. We could go through a season, like everyone does, in which we're seeing less with our physical eyes and more with our spiritual eyes. What will happen to our faith if we no longer see what we're used to seeing?

Our faith is going to be rocked if we're relying on what we're seeing. However, if we're relying on what the Holy Spirit is telling us, then no matter what changes, we have a history with God that will keep us going. When we are in the habit of asking the Holy Spirit what we're seeing while we're seeing it, we are prepared for anything. We're able to know whatever we need to know.

Finally, your question brings up another question: Are the lights, swirls, orbs, or other seemingly metaphysical information captured on camera *always* spiritual? Not necessarily. If the photographer is in a place where there's obviously spiritual activity happening, then what the camera captures is most likely spiritual. But it's easy to fake those orbs, and there could be physical phenomena that are producing points of light. This is why we can't rely on the physical realm to tell us what is happening in the spiritual realm. When camera companies figure out a way to automatically erase the odd lights, orbs, and other elements from our pictures, we don't want our faith to be based on a camera. Instead, we want to rely on the Holy Spirit to tell us what's going on.

CHAPTER 8

SEERS AND GOD'S METAPHORIC LANGUAGE

In Chapter Two, we discussed metaphorical understanding and the "dark speech" of God. He will sometimes speak to us literally, but He *often* speaks through metaphors because they help us see Him more clearly. Metaphors can give us a reference point for understanding who He is, which is the purpose of every communication He has with us. *Come and know Me,* He whispers.

Whenever God communicates with us, He's inviting us deeper into the mystery of who He is. Even if He's telling us something seemingly inconsequential, such as where we lost our car keys, He's letting us know there are things about Him that we never knew before. Every interaction we have with Him is an invitation to see Him in ways we never imagined. After a while, we reach a point in learning God's language where we don't look for what He's saying only; we also look to see what He's *like* as He's saying it, because that makes known who He is.

This continual revelation is not restricted to what He communicates through the seer gifting; it is also true of everything He has ever done, such as creating the universe. It all speaks of Him.

When God scooped up a handful of soil and created the human race, He took part of His nature and breathed it into us. We were created in His image. The result is that we have a definite, tangible *need* to understand His ways, His thoughts, His insight, His language. We are incomplete without Him.

Adam and Eve knew Him face to face. They had relationship with Him at a level most of us can't begin to comprehend. They walked with Him in the Garden the way they walked with each other. The Fall didn't ruin humanity's chance of growing back into communion with God at this level on Earth, but with Adam and Eve's actions, we chose to use the divine deposits instilled within us in any way we wanted. As humans, we have incredible power in both the spiritual and physical realms, and whenever we have incredible power and no relationship with God, we become corrupt. Without God, power will destroy us, even if we begin with good intentions. We were made to live, move, and have our being within Him, so anything within us that doesn't allow room for Him will grow twisted and perverse.

> HE OFTEN SPEAKS THROUGH METAPHORS BECAUSE THEY HELP US SEE HIM MORE CLEARLY.

For Adam and Eve's descendents, the result of being able to do whatever they wanted was the Tower of Babel. God told Adam and Eve to be fruitful and multiply. He reiterated the command to

Noah and his family after the flood: "Fill the earth." However, many of Noah's descendents didn't want to do that. It was much easier for them to stay in the same place and live, work the land, and be in community together, and so that was what they proposed to do:

> They said, "Come, let us build for ourselves a city, and a tower whose top will reach into heaven, and let us make for ourselves a name, otherwise we will be scattered abroad over the face of the whole earth."
> — Genesis 11:4

Most of them agreed to this plan, and in unity they started the tower. They were one language, one people, one set of integrated giftings — giftings that actively worked for them even when the people were in sin (Romans 11:29). They were created to be a single, unified body, and therefore, what the unified body had proposed was going to work. God knew they would be successful unless He stepped in and stopped them.

"We need to scatter them," He said. "Otherwise, they will do everything they put their mind to" (Genesis 11:6–7). So He confused their language. He took the complete language He had given them in the Garden, pulled it apart, and distributed it, sending pieces of it throughout the Earth. Not only did the people end up with different languages, but they also ended up like the pieces of a puzzle; without the others, they were imperfect and limited. They were not a complete body any longer.

Today, we are in this same position. We are not a complete body, and we won't be until we are living in unity. However, as we have discovered multiple times, we cannot achieve such unity our-selves; God is the One who must bring together what He scattered in Genesis.

Throughout the Bible, we see God scattering and re-gathering. He did this with the Israelites multiple times. They would sin and be sent into exile, and after their repentance, He would bring them back. Today, there are nearly seven thousand different languages on Earth, and God doesn't want any of them to be missing from His bride. He is in the process of reuniting everything He distributed — and yet it is not truly about the language. That isn't what God is seeking. Language is simply the processing center for something more important: revelation of Him.

In order to understand any type of communication, we have to be able to process it, and in order to process it, we need language. This means that revelatory gifting cannot be separated from language, and language cannot be separated from revelatory gifting. When God scattered the physical languages in Genesis, He was scattering the revelatory giftings as well.

We see proof of this on a daily basis. Almost every people group in the world has a place for seers: witch doctors, shamans, medicine men, psychics — the list goes on. Clearly, the way they're using the giftings isn't always godly, but where the person is genuine, each of these is the original gifting manifesting itself. Each culture has a different way of using the giftings because each culture has a different piece of it, and each piece is important to God's heart.

At salvation, when God opens the eyes of our hearts and breathes life into our spirits, He doesn't leave our heritage at the door; He doesn't require us to learn a new way of communicating with Him. Instead, He speaks to us the way He created us to be spoken to. We don't need to hear from Him the way other people hear from Him. We need to hear from Him in our own individual way, for that is how He made us.

Each of us possesses a piece of the original gifting He distributed, and no two people have the same piece. Our gifting may *resemble* someone else's, but like our fingerprints, it is unique to us.

As we learn to walk in our giftings, He will use others and their giftings as examples, but His goal is to stimulate *our* giftings in *us*, the giftings that have come down through our bloodlines.

The Bible says that God is returning for every tribe and tongue, but it isn't necessarily just the languages themselves — it is the heart-to-heart communication that each individual language carries. Someday when God takes His bride into the bridal chamber, He doesn't want her to miss any tone, reflection, or posture of His; He wants her to *know* Him. Consequently, He's waiting for her fullness so that she can receive all of who He is. His ways are invested in people all over the globe. Each of us has a part in Him.

ANCIENT HEBREW: GOD'S METAPHORIC LANGUAGE

> *The heavens are telling of the glory of God;*
> *And their expanse is declaring the work of His hands.*
> — Psalm 19:1

God declares His nature in countless ways: how He structures leadership, how He speaks in dreams, how He prophesies, how He heals. He also declares His nature in His Word. It is infallible, yet God let it be written through the hand of man. It was recorded in different languages, yet it still conveys who He is. All of the Bible is utterly astonishing, including the Hebrew language itself.

Hebrew-based languages are the only languages we see God writing with His own hand. He wrote the Ten Commandments in stone for Moses. He wrote on the wall for Belshazzar (Daniel 5); the king's wise men couldn't interpret or even read the writing, so they brought in someone who could: Daniel. When Jesus knelt down and wrote in the dirt (John 8:6), it was very likely that He was writing in Hebrew.

Today, like most modernized languages, Hebrew is written with symbols, but thousands of years ago in the times of Moses and David, Hebrew was a pictographic language similar to Egyptian hieroglyphics. Every symbol was a picture, and the meaning of every word was based on the metaphorical meaning of the pictures. As a result, each word had deep, intrinsic meaning.

Many languages are phonetic, meaning that their speakers use letters to sound out words. Until the King James Bible was printed, English had no set standard for how words were to be spelled; each writer spelled according to his or her interpretation of the sounds. But ancient Hebrew is different. It is not based on how words *sound*; it is based on what words *mean*. Again, when God speaks, both what He speaks and how He speaks are important, and the language of His chosen people reflects that. Consequently, ancient Hebrew gives us profound detail into the ways of God.

If we were literate Hebrews living in ancient times, we would most likely have a general understanding of dreams, metaphors, and other signs simply because we read the language. It would naturally train us in metaphorical understanding and therefore in the way God often communicates.

My interest in ancient Hebrew increased a few years ago when I came across a website that detailed the language's pictographic letters.[1] At the time, I was taking a biblical dream interpretation course. That course ripped apart my traditional thought processes and radically enhanced my relationship with God, because I began to realize that what I was seeing in the spiritual realm had meaning. I was opened to metaphoric understanding. I reasoned, *If what this course is telling us is true, then the symbols it teaches will line up with the symbols and the words in Hebrew.* I didn't doubt the accuracy of the course; I just presumed one would back up the other, which it did at a level I wasn't expecting.

The first word I looked up was *shem*, the Hebrew word for "name." *Shem* is comprised of two pictures: a picture of teeth and a picture of water. Teeth typically represent understanding because we "chew on something" (we think about it, meditate on it) in order to understand it. Water represents spirit or mystery. Ancient Hebrew, therefore, seems to suggest that a person's name is the understanding of his or her mystery or spirit.

This means that when God renamed Peter in John 1, He was naming his spirit. He was explaining the mystery of who the man was and how he was measured. It also means that when Adam named the animals in the Garden, he was not involved in a random

---

1 Ancient Hebrew Research Center - www.ancient-hebrew.org

activity; he wasn't simply making up sounds and piecing together words. He was describing the animals' natures and their functions on the Earth. He was naming what they *were*. There is an incredible authority involved in that.

This same authority is involved when we name our children: We are identifying the calling on their spirit — we are recognizing the reason God breathed life into them. What a profound thing! And how astonishing that God trusts us to do this.

This level of authority shouldn't alarm parents or make them fearful of choosing the wrong names for their kids. God gave us an innate sense of how to do this well. When we find the right name, we know. *That is the one.* Even if we choose a first name solely to honor family or friends, we typically pick the middle name we really want the child to have. How we choose our children's names may be a nonlogical process, but it is usually a careful process.

In ancient Hebrew, *name* can mean the understanding of the spirit: not humanity's understanding but God's understanding.

I have barely brushed the surface of all the different words in ancient Hebrew, but with every one I study, I am blown away by the depth of understanding that comes out of it.

THE NAMES OF GOD

Inherently, the ancient Hebrew language gives us weighty insight into the names and character of God. Perhaps you have come across some of His Hebrew names before at church or in Bible studies. For example:

Elohim (The Strong One)
El Roi (The God Who Sees)
El Shaddai (The All-Sufficient God)
El Elyon (The Most High God)

As you can see in these examples, the root word for "God" in the Old Testament is *El*, which is made up of an ox head and a shepherd's staff; the ox head represents strength because men would plow with oxen, and the shepherd's rod symbolizes authority, rule, and order. So *El*, the root word of "God" in Hebrew, essentially means "strong order." Therefore, when we pray to Him, we're asking that whatever we're praying for would come under that "strong order."

> IN ANCIENT HEBREW, NAME CAN MEAN THE UNDERSTANDING OF THE SPIRIT: NOT HUMANITY'S UNDERSTANDING BUT GOD'S UNDERSTANDING.

God is also our Father. The Hebrew root word for "father" is *ab*, represented by an ox head and a tent. Again, the ox head means "strength," and the tent means "family" or "covering." *Ab* is the strong one, or strong covering, of the family. That is the father's role, and it is God's role for us, in our lives — He is our Strong One, who is capable of covering us and bringing everything in our lives to order. We don't need this to be explained by scholars and theologians; this is what the words themselves seem to say about Him.

When Jesus said that God is His Father, His *Ab*, He confused the Hebrews, because He was saying that God is His covering — His Dad. It's an issue of *family*, because that is what the tent represents.

As you can see, even a short length of time spent studying God's names in their original language could ruin us for anything but a deeply intimate, deeply passionate walk with Him. We would get to know Him in new ways, really know Him, in the language He chose for Himself and His Word.

ANCIENT HEBREW AND SEERS

When I looked up the word "seer," I discovered that there were two words commonly used. The first word, which Samuel was called in 1 Samuel 9, is *ro'eh*, which, of course, means "to see." It describes both seeing in the spiritual and seeing in the natural. The pictographic characters are a human head and an ox head, seeming to mean that what we see is a strong impression.

Ro'eh, however, is not the more common word for "seer" in the Old Testament. The more common word is *chozeh*, which has two characters: *chet*, meaning "tent wall," and *zayin*, meaning a "mattock" or "knife."

The word *chet* is also used for "firmament" in Genesis 1:6–8:

Then God said, "Let there be an expanse in the midst of the waters, and let it separate the waters from the waters."

God made the expanse, and separated the waters which were below the expanse from the waters which were above the expanse; and it was so.

God called the expanse heaven. And there was eve-
ning and there was morning, a second day.

The firmament is a tent wall or divider that must be pierced in order for something to access what is on the other side. Our atmosphere is difficult for outer objects to penetrate; they often incinerate during entry. It is also difficult for inner objects to exit; space shuttles use a significant amount of fuel trying to achieve orbit. In order for something to cross through to the other side, the divider must first be pierced.

> IN ANCIENT HEBREW, *NAME* CAN MEAN THE UNDERSTANDING OF THE SPIRIT: NOT HUMANITY'S UNDERSTANDING BUT GOD'S UNDERSTANDING.

How could a tent wall and a cutting tool represent a seer? These pictographs took me awhile to understand. Then it came to me. Seers *see through* the divide. For them, the division between the physical and the spiritual has been opened. They are the cut in the wall.

Based on the ancient Hebrew language, that seems to be the definition of what it means to be a seer. This gifting pierces the boundary, and through the divide, we receive sensory data from the spiritual realm.

All of us have the ability of seeing through this divide; we have our piece of the original language, and it is an open invitation to look and see what God is doing. However, our giftings are not for us alone; they are also for the benefit of the Church and the world. They are pieces of a puzzle — one that requires every piece in order to be complete.

What does this mean for the Church as a whole? Essentially,

we help one another see through the divide. One way we do this is by sharing what we're seeing — not just *what* we're seeing but also *how* we're seeing it, so that other people's faith to see for themselves will grow.

But at this juncture, many of us have an issue. Sharing what we're seeing and experiencing is not always an easy thing to do. It tends to feel risky and uncomfortable, because we don't know how the other people will respond. Will they reject what we're saying? Will we offend them? Will they think we are strange? *Are* we strange? Being open and sharing with others can be difficult, especially when God speaks to us with analogies and metaphors that seem awkward to repeat or difficult to explain. This leads us to the subject of the next chapter.

Prophetic & Seer Q&A:

QUESTION: How does a psychic differ from a seer? I have met some who say that they have had "experiences" since childhood.

ANSWER: I am going to answer this with a progression of language in Scripture:

> Formerly in Israel, when a man went to inquire of God, he used to say, "Come, and let us go to the seer"; for he who is called a prophet now was formerly called a seer.
> — 1 Samuel 9:9

> Now the boy Samuel was ministering to the LORD before Eli and word from the LORD was rare in those days, visions were infrequent.
> — 1 Samuel 3:1

> When David arose in the morning, the word of the LORD came to the prophet Gad, David's seer.
> — 2 Samuel 24:11

In the first passage, in the phrase "Let us go to the seer," the word *seer* is the Hebrew word *ro'eh*, which ancient Hebrew forms with a picture of a human head and an ox head. This essentially means a strong reception of the head; it is used interchangeably as the root for mystical seeing ("I saw the future") and natural seeing ("I saw Joe today").

The mystical use implies someone who gets impressions or sees things. It doesn't mean he or she does this for God.

Later in that same passage, it says, "For he who is now called a prophet was formerly called a seer." The word *seer* is the same as before, but the word *prophet* here is the Hebrew word *nabiy*. In ancient Hebrew, this root word is formed with a picture of a seed and the picture of a tent. It essentially means sowing seeds into the life of a person or the lives of a group. By connotation, it means speaking words (God's words) into a person or group of people that go into their lives and have the potential to grow and bring forth new fruit.

The shift in language here is significant because it differentiates between people who have spiritual gifts that allow them to receive supernatural impressions and people who are intentionally using their gifts to do God's will. *Ro'eh*, the first word for "seer," doesn't make a distinction between *psychic* and *seer*.

Looking at the second passage, we can make the logical assumption that the reason the "word of the Lord was rare in those days" was that most of the seers weren't using their gifts to hear God's words. This changed when Samuel came along, used his seeing gift for God, and started a school of prophets to teach other seers how to communicate with God as well.

In the third passage where it says, "The word of the Lord came to the prophet Gad, David's seer," the same word for "prophet" is used but a different word for "seer" is used. The Hebrew root word for "seer" in this passage is *chozeh*. It is used almost exclusively for "seer" from here on out. In ancient Hebrew, the pictographs for *chozeh* are a tent wall and a cutting tool. It essentially means having the boundaries between Earth and Heaven cut open. In this case, Gad, a prophet dedicated to speaking God's words into the people, was also David's seer: one who had the boundary cut open into Heaven so he could tell David what he was seeing.

So to answer your question with a summary . . . psychics could be *ro'eh* seers in that they receive impressions in their heads via God-created gifts, but they could never be *chozeh* seers until they dedicate the use of their spiritual gifts to God and God opens Heaven to them. If this were to happen, they would no longer be psychics but prophetic seers.

CHAPTER 9

WHY SHOULD I
SHARE WHAT I *SEE*?

SEERS AND THE ISSUE OF KINDNESS

As you read this book, hopefully it will help you realize how much God is speaking to you personally. He doesn't speak just to the men and women who have reputations for hearing Him, but He speaks to everyone. To the stay-at-home parents who've never even thought of the possibility. To the kids who "make up" stories about talking with Him, only to be told they have great imaginations. To professionals who think they're not spiritual and to teenagers who think they're somehow beyond God's notice. As a minister, it is not my desire to hear from God *for* you; my desire is to convince you that God is already speaking to you. We don't need to dial an operator when we have God's direct line. When we think of it like that, we will be further inspired to press forward and figure out how this works.

In this chapter, we're going to be discussing one of the chief issues that arises for seers: the issue of sharing with others.

THE SHARING DILEMMA

A few years ago, my family and I were attending church one Sunday morning, and God gave me a word for a visitor in the congregation. A visitor, mind you. I saw her as a fat Viking lady, and I strongly felt that God wanted me to tell her what I saw. I was standing in front of the entire congregation, and that was all He directed me to say. If this woman was at all sensitive about her weight, I was going to find myself in a highly awkward situation. This required a substantial step of faith from me.

I told her what God wanted me to say, and then — only then — did He give me more to say. The gist of the word was that it wasn't over until the fat lady sang. I later learned the woman was going through a divorce.

It isn't always easy to be open and transparent with what God has shown us, because it forces us out of our comfort zones and can leave us feeling foolish — not necessarily *being* foolish, but certainly *feeling* that way. As in the story I just related to you, there have been times when God gave me only a sentence or just a partial picture, and I knew that He wanted me to speak it to the relevant person or group before He would give me the rest of the word. Depending on the circumstances, it

> It isn't always easy to be OPEN and transparent with what God has SHOWN us, because it forces us out of our comfort ZONES.

can take a good deal of faith to do that. Sometimes, I know He wants me to describe in detail exactly what I'm seeing for the person or persons, but what I'm seeing isn't something that I'd ever want to say in front of strangers, possibly even in front of friends. God doesn't have the same social boundaries we do, and occasionally, the seer gifting will accentuate that.

Here is another example. Some years ago, I went on a ministry trip with my pastor and a mutual friend. We were up late talking one night, and one of them asked me, "What's the weirdest thing that's ever happened to you?"

That can be an uncomfortable question for a seer. I felt God say to me, *Tell them about My names.* That was not a story I was comfortable sharing at the time, but I knew that God wanted me to, so I began.

According to Jewish folklore, God has a seventy-two-character name only the Judaic high priests know. At the time, I had been studying the sevenfold Spirit of God portrayed in Isaiah 11:2: the Spirit of the Lord, Spirit of wisdom, Spirit of understanding, Spirit of counsel, Spirit of might, Spirit of knowledge, and Spirit of the fear of the Lord. The sevenfold Spirit is also mentioned numerous times in Revelation. As I considered the secret seventy-two-character name of God, something struck me as strange. Caiaphas, the high priest who sentenced Jesus to death, had been entrusted with the seventy-two-character name of God.

How could You trust him with that? I asked. *He killed Your Son. How could You trust him with Your name?*

In response, I felt the Lord say to me, *I can protect My name. You think I wouldn't be able to protect My name? I can protect My name.*

Something else occurred to me. If God has a seventy-two-character name, perhaps the sevenfold Spirit of God has seven secret names of God as well.

The moment I thought that, I felt a heat come on my head, and I knew that if I opened my mouth, I could speak aloud the seven secret names of the sevenfold Spirit of God.

Immediately, I clearly sensed an angel beside me.

"What are you doing here?" I asked him.

"I'm here to stop you from saying those names," he replied. He was carrying a wide sword that was sheathed in dark leather.

"What does that mean?"

He looked at me. Matter-of-factly, he said, "What do you think it means?"

I knew that if I tried to say the names, he would strike me, but I wasn't sure if his strike would kill me, remove the knowledge, or simply hinder my ability to speak. For weeks, the sensation of being able to speak the secret names of God stayed with me, and this angel with the wide sword followed me around. I was tempted to find out what would happen if I tried to say the names, but I didn't.

That is the story I shared with them, because God had impressed me to do so and because they were open to believe it. I had favor with them. Favor can be a dangerous thing, for it allows people to believe what you say and to respond to it. When I was done with this story, these men certainly responded.

"Wow, Jim," they told me. "You need to get some real friends, because we can't be your friends. We like you, but we can't even remotely identify with you enough to be your friend, and if you don't have friends, you will die because you'll be all alone."

That night, I stayed awake for a long time and thought about what they'd said. Over time, I realized that they were right; it had been godly counsel. I was trying to conform myself to the circle I was in, and I was growing more and more alone. My favor with the people and my faith were both growing, but the gifting rested solely on me. I was the one who decided if something was too strange to share or not, and if I decided the latter, then I wouldn't share it. I would keep the *chet*, the divide, in place.

Later, when my wife and I were leaving that church, the pastor told me, "You were the safety. You were the firewall. Everything you did was fine and safe, because you kept it fine and safe."

Unfortunately, he was right, in more ways than one. I hadn't shared the truly weird and bizarre elements with the church; as a congregation, we had been given an invitation to come and know God and His mystery at a deeper level, but I personally hadn't responded, because I knew the pastor wouldn't have a grid for a lot of the things I was seeing. In the end, I realized that he and I had not been fully co-laboring. I had not helped the people around me to see through the divide and participate fully in what God wanted to do through me.

WHY IS SHARING IMPORTANT?

Something happens in the spiritual realm when a person is willing to be thought peculiar for God. It can lower walls. It can open doors that have previously been closed. When we are willing to describe what we're seeing to others, it releases them into interacting with God and seeing His spiritual realities for themselves.

I find that whenever I share the strange things I'm seeing, people come out of the woodwork with even stranger things. I listen to their stories and think, *That is pretty unusual. I can sense it's of God — but I've never seen anything like that.* Their faith then increases mine and vice versa.

The concept of sharing with others took on new meaning for me when I did a word study on *kindness*. When I looked it up in ancient Hebrew, I was puzzled by what I found. The Hebrew word for *kindness* is composed of thorns, a wall, and a door.

Initially, that doesn't sound kind at all. To confuse the matter even more, the same base word for *kindness* is sometimes used for *rejection*! How could something associated with rejection possibly mean kindness as well?

But then, God gave me some insight.

Kindness is the open door in the wall.

THE WALL COVERED WITH THORNS

In order to really understand the meaning of *kindness* and what it has to do with seers, we need to understand walls, or boundaries. The importance of personal boundaries has become a popular topic in Christian circles. Simply defined, they help delineate who we are, what we have authority over, and what belongs to us. They protect what we deem sacred and also define relationship: Those we trust are permitted inside the boundary, while those we don't are kept at a distance. Anything that crosses the boundary without permission aggravates us and provokes us to defend ourselves.

As all of us have experienced, there are many people who have little concept of the boundaries of others. They break through the wall and violate our personal space without realizing they've intruded.

"I'm going to stay for dinner."

"I'm going to borrow your car tonight."

"I know you just loaned me money last week, but something's come up, and I need to borrow more."

"I need you to watch the kids again. Thanks."

Once or twice we may not resent requests such as these, but if our friends or acquaintances take our boundaries for granted and keep doing so, in order to survive, we'll eventually realize that they don't have a right to expect us to help them all the time — especially if the requests never stop. *Wait a minute. I already gave that to them once. I already gave it to them two or three times. If I don't ever tell them, "No," they'll just keep asking.*

> THERE ARE TIMES WHEN WE NEED TO BE CARED FOR... BUT NONE OF US HAVE THE RIGHT TO ASSUME THAT WE AREN'T RESPONSIBLE FOR OUR LIVES, THAT OTHERS WILL TAKE CARE OF US.

Respecting boundaries, both our own and those of others, is imperative for all relationships. There are times when we need to be cared for, provided for, held up, held accountable, etc., but none of us have the right to assume that we aren't responsible for our lives, that others will take care of us. As it is with blind spots, a lot of people who struggle with boundaries don't realize they struggle with them, and consequently, they tend to drain their friends and family members. They burn them out and then don't understand why many of their relationships end poorly.

Here is where kindness comes into play. If we cross a boundary that hasn't been opened to us, we're forcing ourselves into a restricted area. This is one reason Jesus said in John 10:1 that he who comes over the wall is a thief and a robber. In order to be properly admitted into someone's private circle, we have to be invited in. We have to use the door.

That is my understanding of the Hebrew meaning of kindness — inviting people through the boundary and into what they couldn't enter on their own.

THE DOOR

God told the Israelites to be kind to strangers because they were once strangers themselves (Exodus 22:21). "Strangers" are on the outside, on the other side of our boundaries, and we can show them the kindness of God by inviting them in. They don't have a right to force themselves into our lives; they can't demand to be allowed into our community, but we can open the door and *let them* in. Kindness means inclusion. It is giving people access to something they have no hope of obtaining unless it is given to them.

The entirety of our faith is based upon kindness. We had deep, personal, face-to-face relationship with God in the Garden, but when Adam and Eve sinned, intimacy with God at that level on Earth ended. In that instance, the dividing wall and its thorns was an angel with a flaming sword (Genesis 3:24). Thousands of years later, Jesus willingly went to the cross so that His Father could be kind to us and invite us back into intimacy with Him — a relationship we are not able to force or achieve on our own.

As seers, we have our lives, our thoughts, our hopes, our dreams, our spiritual experiences, and the revelation God has given us. Kindness is when we invite people to share those with us. In our community are people we love and trust, and kindness is when we ask them into fellowship and relationship with us — not just to sit next to us at church, but into our relationships and into our lives, where we share with them. Our faith increases theirs, and theirs, in turn, increases ours.

As we discussed in Chapter Eight, ancient Hebrew seems to define *seer* as a cut in the wall. Therefore, as we're led by God to share what we are seeing with others, we are exemplifying His kindness because we're allowing them through the boundary to partake in the mystery on the other side. Again, every person is potentially capable of seeing in the spiritual realm. We don't share only when we are more talented or more capable than others; we share because God is issuing an invitation that is pertinent to all involved.

> THE HEBREW WORD FOR *KINDNESS* IS COMPOSED OF THORNS, A WALL, AND A DOOR... KINDNESS IS THE OPEN DOOR IN THE WALL.

When I realized what kindness truly meant, I became much more willing to share what I was seeing. If I have to feel uncomfortable in front of an individual, the pastor, or a church, but in the process, I am able to demonstrate God's nature and invite people to participate in what He's doing — that's worth it. In fact, that's worth being terrified as a child because I was seeing things that frightened me, and it's worth years and years of not understanding who, or what, I was. If you are reading this book, you likely experienced similar hardships. Something happens inside of us when we are willing to be kind. We discover that we're not just inviting other people inside our boundaries; we're inviting *God* inside our boundaries. We are asking for more of Him in our lives. We begin to take on His likeness.

He has put an urge to be kind in our spirits; our giftings want to share what they sense is happening around them. We were designed to want to interact with the spiritual realm and see God's will come to pass and to help others do the same.

SEER PITFALLS

If part of our responsibility as seers is to show kindness by including others in the hidden dealings of God, we violate that responsibility when we are exclusive in our giftings.

Each of us has the ability to experience the spiritual realm, but exclusivity assumes, *Because I can do this, I am special; therefore, everyone else should consider me valuable.* This is an easy hole for seers to stumble into, and we sometimes find it with good intentions.

For example, a common way seers exclude others is by giving backhanded advice. A few years ago, I was driving down the highway and saw some turkeys along the side of the road. My boys were in the car with me, so I said, "Look at those turkeys."

They started exclaiming, "Wow! Turkeys, Dad! Can we stop and catch one? Let's eat it!" (Boys will be boys.)

I saw the turkeys and pointed them out so that my sons could see them, too. I would not have been kind if, to teach them a lesson, I hadn't mentioned the turkeys until later: "I saw turkeys back there. Do you know why you didn't? Because you don't pay attention. Next time, you need to do better." Our objective in saying something like that could be sincere — we really do want to help others grow in their giftings, but what we're actually doing is highlighting our apparent success and their apparent failure, which does not accurately represent God's nature.

Similarly, another way seers commonly exclude others is when we insinuate that we can see better than they can. "I received revelation from God, and the way I received it was extraordinary, but you wouldn't understand because you don't have the level of experience I do." If we don't describe what we're seeing in such a way that others can "see" it for themselves, the result is that we appear to be unusually spiritual. I've caught myself doing something similar before with dream interpreters who were using Stir the Water's dream interpretation training site.[1] My goal was to help them become better interpreters, but I would tell them what I knew the dream meant without helping them understand how they could arrive at the same answer. "Your interpretation needs to look like this," I would say, and they would go away discouraged because I hadn't actually helped them. When I realized this, I altered my methods. I began to emphasize what they were doing well and then telling them how they could do better. That greatly improved the results of the training site.

When we share what we're seeing with others — whether

---

1 For more information about www.stirthewater.com/dreams, see Appendix 2.

that be the entire church, our small group, or just a friend — we need to share it in such a way that God can give that person or group revelation about it, too, even though they weren't the ones to see it originally. By doing this, we are helping them touch an aspect of God that they've potentially never been able to touch before, and there is great reward in that. There is life in that, both for them and for us.

ENTERING BY THE GATE

As I mentioned before, I've been a hardnosed introvert my entire life. My wife is an extrovert. She and I once took a personality test together, and she answered every question as an extrovert, and I answered every question as an introvert. As you may imagine, there has been a certain amount of conflict in our marriage based on these differences.

For instance, after we were married, Mims would ask me, "What are you thinking?"

"What do you want to know for?" I'd reply.

"I want to know what you're thinking. We never talk about what you're thinking."

"Well, they're my thoughts."

I was not being kind, and for good reason, she was not respecting my boundaries; she was pushing to know me better, and I wanted to control the information she received.

If we need to get through the wall in front of us but can't find the door, we will often attempt to get over the boundary in any way we can. We will bash it in, climb it, burn it down, or do whatever needs to be done in order for us to get through to the other person. Many times, we feel justified in doing this, because the other person is our spouse, parent, child, or friend, and naturally we need to be near him or her. My wife had every right to be included in my life, but I had not left a door for her.

The door is at the center of relationship. Its presence shows others that eventually, it may be possible for them to enter here. They may not be permitted to pass through right away, but they have hope for the future, and in the meantime, they don't have to force the relationship to happen. If seers don't leave a way for others to enter in after them, it encourages those who have a God-given desire to interact with the spiritual realm to become thieves. This occurs with spiritually gifted Christians and spiritually gifted non-Christians as well, both of whom attract like-minded people by the score.

> THOSE OF US WHO SURVIVE FIND A PLACE TO BELONG; WE GAIN WISDOM AND DISCOVER THAT THERE ARE OTHERS WHO HUNGER FOR GOD AS WE DO.

At its core, the seer gifting is essentially an evangelistic function. How? Because it invites people into the work of God, which is the heart of evangelism: telling people the good news and letting them know that they can have it, too. It isn't good news if we don't let them know how they can have it as well.

The kindness of God can be applied to more than just the seer gifting; it can also apply to spiritual and emotional wandering. All of us have gone through times of feeling alone and misunderstood. As the Israelites did in Egypt, we have felt like aliens in a strange land. Those of us who survive find a place to belong; we gain wisdom and discover that there are others who hunger for God as we do. We become residents, and we are aliens no longer. Kindness is what allows this to happen.

When we open the door for others, we become catalysts for great things of God.

BALAAM AND THE SEER
Numbers 22–25, 31:16; Revelation 2:14

It is *good* to cooperate with what God is doing. It fills us with His peace; refreshes our spirits; and allows us to rediscover that yes, He is good, even if we don't fully understand His plan or His ways. The world changes when courageous men and women decide to lay down their own devices and cooperate with the plans of Heaven.

We can cooperate with God both intuitively and intentionally. Walking in our seer giftings helps us do the latter. It helps us stay in sync with Him. He greatly desires to direct our steps and show us His heart, but if we have no sense of what He's doing, we may be trying to do the opposite.

Balaam is a biblical example of someone who missed what God was doing. You probably know the Old Testament story. For lack of a better term, Balaam was a "prophetic mercenary" who was hired by King Balak to put a hit on Israel. The first time the king made his request, God told Balaam not to go. Balaam obeyed and sent the men away. But Balak was persistent, and when he sent men a second time, God told Balaam, "All right, go — but say only what I tell you to say."

Early the next morning, Balaam got up, saddled his donkey,

and started off down the road. This is where the story becomes a little out of the ordinary.

God knew the intent of Balaam's heart. Angry at why the man was going, God sent the Angel of the Lord to oppose him. Balaam couldn't see the angel, but his donkey could, and when she refused to go near it, Balaam became upset and started beating her.

This happened three times. In the middle of the third beating, the Lord opened the donkey's mouth, and she turned to Balaam and asked, "Why are you beating me?"

If Balaam was surprised that a donkey was speaking to him, Scripture doesn't reveal it. "Because you're making a fool of me!" he replied. "If I had a sword, I would kill you!"

"Do I normally act like this?" she demanded. "Is this normal behavior for me?"

"Well . . . no." Then Balaam's eyes were opened, and he saw the angel with the sword standing there, planning on killing him if he continued. The donkey had saved his life.

Clearly, a purpose of Heaven was going on. God was revealing His ways on the Earth, but it wasn't the prophet who functioned as the seer here — it was the donkey. When the donkey spoke, she alluded to something beyond Balaam's understanding, which caused Balaam to look and see the angel. In essence, she opened the door and invited him to see into the purposes of Heaven. Once Balaam looked and realized that the current purpose of Heaven was to be certain he didn't curse the Israelites, even if it meant killing him, he was suddenly motivated to participate with God.

Balaam responded to the donkey's invitation to see into the

spiritual realm, yet he did not respond with his whole heart. When he arrived at his destination, he obeyed God's direct order and did not curse Israel. Instead, he blessed the people three times, which greatly offended his employer. But then the contract prophet showed his true colors. He knew that God did not want him to curse the Israelites, but he desired to please the man paying him, so he found a loophole that would enable the curse to take place anyway.

He told the king, "I'm not allowed to curse them, but if you send your pretty young daughters down with their gods and they get married to their sons and lead them off into idolatry, God will curse them for you. You won't need me to do it." And that was what happened.

Balaam's donkey is often used as an example of how easy it is to prophesy: "If a donkey can do it, you can do it, too." But she's also a good example of being a seer. She invited Balaam to grow closer to God, to learn His heart and His ways, which he ended up refusing to do. We know this because at the end of the story, he really hadn't changed.

Seers don't always need to be purposeful about sharing with others. In certain situations, we may not even realize we're sharing. We just need to be *open* and kind so that we can experience God together.

The donkey invited the prophet to realize what was going on, so that he could interact with Heaven. And by all means, if a donkey can help others see into the spiritual realm, so can we.

PROPHETIC & SEER Q&A:

QUESTION: I witnessed something several months ago that disturbed me. I wonder if you can shed light on it. A well-known prophet gave a four-day teaching, and on the last night, he gave a word that humiliated, cursed, and damaged a person in public. I never knew God to do that, and it is not in the Bible anywhere. I don't think this person was a false prophet but do think there was something very wrong with the delivery. Can you explain? I have a few ideas on what can cause that and really need confirmation. Thank you!

ANSWER: When looking at a situation like this, it is very important to keep certain things separate: the gift to receive revelation, the anointing on the gift, what God is doing, and the choices the speaker is making. All of these affect what goes on during ministry.

First, the revelatory gift allows us to receive revelation. That revelation can come from God, the demonic, creation, or other people. As the Bible says, the gift is given irrespective of repentance, which means that the gift can be used and/or misused in many ways.

Second, God's anointing empowers the gift to be used for a purpose. If the gift is like a lamp, then the anointing is the oil that fuels it. As it is with the gift, we have the ability to use the anointing in a partially or fully wrong way.

Although we don't realize it in the moment, we are rarely one hundred percent aligned with God's will. Most of us think we're doing something completely in His will when we're actually only in the ten to sixty percent range. Jesus is the only person to live His whole life, one hundred percent of it, in God's will, and He also may be the only One who has successfully done it for more than a mere moment in time. In God's eyes, our falling short isn't a problem, because we are called to mature and develop. Going from eight to nine percent in God's will is a cause for joy, just as going from seventy-nine to seventy-seven percent is a cause for repentance.

What determines our alignment with God's perfect will? Our choices — both the ones we make intentionally (with full awareness) and the ones we don't make intentionally. We make these choices based on our understanding, our emotions, and our will.

To apply all this to the situation you shared, it is entirely possible that this person, who may be consistently in God's will with how he uses his gift and anointing, made a bad choice in the moment. You'll never know what that bad choice was unless God tells you, so setting that aside, your main role is most likely to pray for two things: Pray for healing for the recipient and pray also that the prophetic person recognizes his wrong choice so he can make a better choice in the future. Pray with humility, because all of us are capable of making similar bad choices based on our own shortcomings and blind spots.

CHAPTER 10

HOW DOES PRAYER AFFECT THE SPIRITUAL REALM?

SEERS AND THE DEMAND OF HEAVEN

"'Your kingdom come.
Your will be done,
On earth as it is in heaven.'"
— Matthew 6:10

I grew up in a small Presbyterian church and learned the Lord's Prayer at an early age. Part of it used to confuse me. Why would we pray for God's will to be done on Earth "as it is in Heaven"? When I was a boy, I thought that must mean He had two wills; He had a list of things to be done in Heaven and then a second, separate list that we should pray to be done on Earth. Jesus, however, was actually saying that the Father's will is established and de-

161

clared in Heaven *before* it is established and declared here: "Your will be done on Earth *as it is* in Heaven."

Why is this important to understand? Because God affects us. His ways, His nature, His character, His desires, and everything else that is of Him and through Him and for Him have an impact on us and on the spiritual realm. They affect the Earth and its inhabitants. This means that when He desires to do something, that desire generates an urgency or demand in the spiritual realm for His will to be done. Depending on the nature of the demand, our individual callings, and our sensitivity to God, our spirits pick up on this urge and begin to perceive that something needs or is about to change, though we may not be able to see or sense it clearly.

This is what I call the demand of Heaven, and it is brought about by the Father's will and our responses to the burdens He has given us. When our prayers align with God's purposes, what we have prayed begins to affect the spiritual realm around us. It is similar to filling a balloon with helium; the increasing pressure inside the balloon brings change to the balloon itself. The latex stretches. Tension builds. As that pressure grows, the atmosphere of the spiritual realm (what we have prayed for) begins to affect the atmosphere of the natural realm (what is happening in the physical), and the two differing pressures attempt to equalize. As it is with the balloon, this creates a certain amount of "tension" in our lives.

Seers can be very sensitive to the ebb and flow of the Spirit, which means that we often are among the first to sense that God desires to do something. We sense the need for change or that something is about to change, but we don't always recognize what that something is. This is *external* pressure; it is coming from outside us.

We will also face *internal* pressure, because God made our giftings and our spirits eager to fulfill Heaven's request. This means that depending on our level of submission to Him, we desire to do His will. Our spirits want to be with Him, doing what He is doing. When He presents His desire to us, our spirits leap, and somewhere within us, we sense an agreement — a longing, even, because we were created to be in union with Him, and we will be restless until our hearts rest in Him.[1]

However, we can learn to ignore both the external and internal pressures, just as we often learn to ignore the seer gifting. How many gifted people have you met who don't seem to be doing anything with their lives? They are brilliant and talented, yet they spend their days in front of the television or dedicate themselves to occupations that don't seem in line with the desires God has given them. Seers sense the external

> WE WILL ALSO FACE INTERNAL PRESSURE, BECAUSE GOD MADE OUR GIFTINGS AND OUR SPIRITS EAGER TO FULFILL HEAVEN'S REQUEST.

pressures of Heaven and are compelled by our very composition to respond to them, but how is it that so many of us are able to disregard what God is directing us to do?

In order to answer this question, allow me to give you another visual. Steve, a seer, is sitting in the window seat of a plane flying at a high altitude. At his shoulder is one of the small double-paned windows that protect the people aboard from the ex-

---

1 St. Augustine, 354–430 A.D.

treme pressure outside the plane. Should something happen to the window, the internal and external pressures would rapidly and abruptly attempt to equalize.

If nothing changed in this situation, no difference in pressure would ever be felt, but there is a small crack in the window next to Steve. It currently isn't large enough to cause significant change; however, he can feel the building tension. The internal and external pressures are attempting to equalize, and he's very aware that *something* wants to change, though he may not be able to sense what that something is.

One of the main issues we as seers experience is that many of the other people aboard the plane don't realize there is a crack in the window. They don't recognize that something wants to change. In fact, they believe that the only sphere of existence is that aboard the plane; therefore, there couldn't be any air exchange because there is no such thing as outside the plane. So they go about their business and continue as normal. Steve's window is about to burst — in other words, change is certainly coming — but most people aren't paying attention.

Here, Steve is faced with two choices. He either can deal with the reality of the window, or he can deal with the reality of the other passengers. The latter choice is much easier, and this is the first step most of us take. We convince ourselves that the crack in the window doesn't exist, that God isn't asking us to do anything beyond what we've tried before, and we attempt to act like normal passengers who are oblivious to the powerful force waiting to approach.

The other choice — accepting the reality of the window —

means venturing into the outer unknown and taking the risks God presents to us. We may not succeed, and we aren't guaranteed safety, but we will be responding to the demand of Heaven and manifesting God's ways and His nature on the Earth.

These external and internal pressures cause seers to live in varying states of mental and spiritual affliction. Some of us understand what's going on, but we choose to ignore it; we decide to overlook the divine whisper that encourages us to try something we have never tried before. Others of us have no idea why we feel such restlessness, and therefore the pressure is worse, because it is heightened by frustration. We sense we should be doing something, but we don't know what or how to make the pressure alleviate. Then there are those of us who understand what's going on and try to adjust to the divine reality "outside the plane." We choose to step into the new thing God has for us, even if we don't fully understand it in the moment.

All of us feel just as strange and have just as hard a time fitting in, but one group has a sense of purpose in life; the other groups are just frustrated, because they're not walking in the fullness of their giftings or destinies.

This is the demand of Heaven. God's desire comes and sits heavily in the spiritual realm, but the world doesn't acknowledge it, and caught between the two, seers try to find balance.

The tragedy is that sometimes, we spend years praying for God's will to be done — for Him to bring revival, for our children to start walking with Him, for our cities, and for our churches — but we don't always understand that when He gives us what we've been asking for, it puts a demand on someone or perhaps several people, and their responses to that demand may be greater than our human comprehension. This means that the actions they decide to take may not align with our expectations. In fact, at times, their actions may even seem to *oppose* what we were praying for, and then, if we are not sensitive to the Holy Spirit, we could end up resisting God, because we don't understand that He supports the actions of this unlikely person or group of people. We may have been the ones who asked that the demand of Heaven come and sit on those people in the first place.

MOSES AND THE DEMAND ON HIS GENERATION

The resolution to the demand of Heaven does not always come into play right away. As most of us realized long ago, God answers our prayers in accordance with His will and timing, not our own. Sometimes, change seems to come immediately; we pray, and God responds within hours, if not minutes. At other times, however, seeing God's will come to pass can be a process filled with pain and frustration, one that takes years to bear fruit.

In the Israelites' case, it took four centuries. Long before Jacob went with his family to Egypt, God told Abraham that his descendants would endure four hundred years of slavery and then return to the Promised Land. His will was released in Heaven, but the Israelites had to cry out for it for four centuries. That was how long it took for His will to take shape on Earth and then be carried out.

In the meantime, it caused some incredible tension. Think about it: the demand of Heaven and *four hundred years* of prayer prayed desperately by an entire nation. That is a significant pressure, and some hapless, gifted man named Moses came along and got stuck right in the middle of it. He was caught up in the suction because his gifting and the calling on his generation were to bring deliverance to God's people.

Just as God has a unique plan for each individual, He has a plan for each generation as well, and that generation puts a demand on its members to walk in it. For instance, in order for Abraham's descendants to be slaves in Egypt for four hundred years, they had to get to Egypt in the first place, so there was a demand on a generation to take them there. Jacob himself wasn't called to take his family into Egypt; it was the demand on his children's generation. Some of them did it as vessels of honor, and some of them did it as vessels of dishonor, but either way, it was done. Joseph felt the pull; he had dreams and listened to God. His brothers also felt the pull and responded by selling Joseph into slavery. Much to their surprise, they later found themselves on their knees before him.

> ...GOD ANSWERS OUR PRAYERS IN ACCORDANCE WITH HIS WILL AND TIMING, NOT OUR OWN.

It was the demand on their generation to move to Egypt and the demand on Moses' generation to bring the people out of Egypt. The problem was that Moses was the only male of his generation who made it to adulthood. The rest were killed by Pharaoh. The anointing and the calling on the men of Moses' generation, therefore, had nowhere else to go except on Moses because none of the others made it. He was the only male recipient available for the demand of Heaven and the burden of four hundred years of prayer. There were other generations present during his time, but they had different callings.

Whenever the demand of Heaven is discussed, a question automatically arises: How can we recognize it in our own lives, both on an individual and generational level? First, we need to understand that God created destiny to be walked in, not to be an allusive, mystical thing floating just beyond our reach. We won't always have a precise understanding of the demand, or demands, of Heaven that God has put upon us, but when we are in a place of trusting Him to lead us, we will likely find ourselves on the right road. That being the case, we can ask ourselves certain questions: What are we interested in doing? What drives us? What do we feel passionate about? What are the leaders from our generation talking about? What isn't being done that needs to be done? What is our generation trying to address, even poorly or negatively? The answers to these questions can be very revealing.

Again, the most important thing we could ever do is just be with Jesus. We can bring our questions to God — questions of destiny, of prayer, of fear and concern — and fully expect Him to answer them for us. He wants us to succeed even more than we do. The enemy has worked hard to convince us that we're lucky to get any sort of answer from Him, but luck has nothing to do with it.

Perhaps you have been able to see the weight of God on your generation playing out in your own life. I believe I have seen it in mine. I was born in 1973 about a month after Roe v. Wade, and I had a very lonely childhood. Outside of my family, I had few friends growing up. I realize that part of this was because I was an unusual child. On top of being affected by my gifting, I would make statements that I didn't think about beforehand and blunder into awkward situations and seemingly make them worse. Those are all factors, but I am convinced that I didn't have very many friends growing up because several of them didn't make it out of the womb. Many of the ones called to be my peers, and possibly yours, are not here.

This means that the demand of Heaven and the weight of all the prayers prayed by previous generations for this generation are heavy upon us — heavier, perhaps, than they would have been, for there are fewer of us.

CHAPTER 11

SEERS AND INTERCESSION

Not too long after my family and I moved to New Hampshire, I felt like God told me to go pray on the Pinnacle, a local mountain dedicated to the purpose of prayer.

Now, it was the end of January, and the end of January in New Hampshire is like the end of the world in other states. It was my first real winter up there, and the snowplow left piles in my driveway that reached up to the basketball hoop. When I tried hiking up the mountain, the snow was so deep that I couldn't see my legs, and after about five steps, I thought, *I'm really tired. I think I'll go home.*

Clearly, if I was going to brave the elements and pray on the mountain, I would have to be serious about it. So I went to the store and bought snowshoes. The first time out with them, I realized they were too small — they didn't keep me on top of the snow. However, I did stop sinking all the way up to my hips. Now I sank only to the middle of my calves, which was much easier!

I would battle my way to the top of the mountain, pray for God's will, and then come back down. I did that all through February. It was one of the most exhausting things I've ever done. Snowshoeing uphill is *hard*. Occasionally, one of my snowshoes would get stuck or fall off, and I think God arranged those little breaks to spare me from having a heart attack! Every time I returned to the car, I would have icicles as thick as my little finger in my beard. I would be drenched in sweat, even though it was well below freezing out there, with an added wind chill.

I did that nearly every day for two months. The snow finally began melting in March, and when the hike started getting easier, you know what happened? God lifted the burden. I knew He didn't need me to pray on the mountain anymore.

"God," I said to Him, "what was that?" I'd had a clear impression to do this, but then the burden had completely lifted.

Do I understand why God wants to do what He wants to do? Not always. Does it make sense to me? Sometimes. Do I look a little strange while I'm doing it? Occasionally. But if I don't see it through, it eats at my peace. It makes me restless. It's a divine pressure: the demand of Heaven that God has placed upon me.

It is the same with you. His ways are not our ways and His thoughts are not our thoughts, so there isn't much possibility that we will consistently appear "normal" to other people. In the world's eyes, we will look strange at times, because that is how they see Him.

Many seers have responded to the intercessory call and intervene on others' behalf through prayer. They *see* (sometimes literally; sometimes it's a sense or an urge) what God is doing in Heaven, and they pray it into existence on Earth. Seeing in the spiritual realm gives us the opportunity to interact with the spiritual realm, and intercession is a significant interaction.

It can also be a difficult interaction. A few years ago as I was preparing to teach on the mechanics of faith, hope, and love and how these work with prayer and intercession, God gave me a picture to help illustrate what is on His heart concerning this. I saw someone struggling up a hill with a bag of rocks on his back. God pointed out how hard the path was. He pointed out that the rocks were heavy, the road was slanted, and that actually reaching the top was something of a feat. Then He gave me understanding. He said that the person carrying the bag already knows that the rocks are heavy, the way is slanted, and that it's hard to get to the top. The people who aren't engaged in intercession are the ones who need the explanation. Otherwise, they might hinder or diminish what the intercessors are trying to do.

> IN THE WORLD'S EYES, WE WILL LOOK STRANGE AT TIMES, BECAUSE THAT IS HOW THEY SEE HIM.

Intercession is a serious calling. It is a larger, more intense commitment than most of us realize. Intercessors are not simply people who pray a lot; they literally wage war on others' behalf. They "see" what God is doing in the spiritual realm — how He is increasing our anointing, how He is opening doors for us, the favor He's about to pour out in our lives, the struggles that have been set in our way — and they take hold of God's promises for us and carry our destinies until we're ready enough and strong enough to carry them ourselves. Their prayers are powerful and help to enact change in our lives.

This is often why intercessors can sometimes seem a little strange; carrying others' burdens puts a strain on them, and, as it is with seers, what God wants to do may not always be what the intercessors would choose to do. They may make some odd decisions and say some odd things, because God has asked them to — for your sake. For my sake. For the pastor's sake. For the church. Intercessors carry great weights for other people, and the reason they push on is that they are committed to seeing us walk into our destinies. They are committed to doing what God has set before them to do: warring for the lives of others. Not all of them understand what they're doing and none of them is perfect in this, but God often asks them for this level of commitment.

Do you see why intercession is a calling? No one could do this without being called. It can be a hard road, and as I travel and speak on the seer gifting and dream interpretation, I meet many intercessors who have been worn out or embittered along the way, frequently because the very people they're interceding for and petitioning God for haven't understood them. Traditionally speaking, the Church doesn't always easily accept intercessors because we find it difficult to accept anything we don't understand. As seers, we are probably familiar with this fact.

INTERCESSION: FAITH, HOPE, AND LOVE

While I was researching this topic of intercession, God highlighted the following passage to me:

We give thanks to God always for you all, making mention of you in our prayers, remembering without ceasing your **work** *of faith,* **labor** *of love, and* **patience** *of hope in our Lord Jesus Christ in the sight of our God and Father.*

— 1 Thessalonians 1:2–3, NKJV, *emphasis mine*

After I read that, I thought, *That sounds like a lot of hard work!* And it is; intercession is truly a labor of love. *Patience* is a nice, clean little word. At first glance, it may not seem like an overly difficult virtue, but another term for patience is *long-suffering,* and *long-suffering* is an adequate description of what intercessors sometimes go through. In order to be successful, they must have the patience of hope.

In ancient Hebrew, the two pictographs composing the root word of *hope* are very simple. The first is a picture of a setting sun, which denotes the passage of time, and the other is a picture of someone who is waiting or looking to receive. That seems to be the biblical definition of hope: someone who is waiting to receive, even if it takes time.

The pictographs of the base word of *faith* are fairly simple as well. They are an ox head, water, and a seed. Again, the ox head means "strength," and the water means "spirit" or "mystery"; the seed represents itself. God gave me revelation, and I began to see that faith implants within us a strong spiritual seed — something that grows.

The pictographs symbolizing the base word of *love* are an

ox head, someone seeing something, and a tent. The picture of the person seeing represents, obviously, something that can be seen, and the tent represents family or inclusion. In other words, love is strong, demonstrative, and involves inclusion or covenant with someone. When we love someone, it isn't weak; it is clear and visible, and it desires to make an eternal commitment to the object of its affection.

This is why, over time, love can be distinguished from infatuation. Though our interest and feelings may be strong when we're infatuated, there is not a lasting urge to make a permanent commitment, so our feelings may or may not evolve into anything of greater depth. But when we truly love someone, our love turns that person into family because we want him or her included in our lives and every good thing we have. God does not do anything without love (1 John 4:16). Therefore, everything He does, He does in order to cause permanent relationship with us.

Love is the basis of intercession. It is an issue of faith, which is receiving strong spiritual seed that eventually bears fruit; it is an issue of hope, which waits for God's promise to come about; and it is an issue of love, which has a strong commitment to seeing others enter what God has for them. By far, the most difficult of these is love, and it is also the greatest (1 Corinthians 13:1–2).

Jesus stressed this as well. He said that His people will do great miracles, cast out demons, and show His power to the world, but at the judgment, He will have to shut the door to many of them, because they don't know Him. In other words, some of us have yet to venture fully into this often painful, consistently wonderful, fulfilling, perfect thing called love.

As I was studying faith, hope, love, and intercession, God again brought Moses to mind. We can see each of these four elements in his life.

MOSES AND THE SEED OF FAITH

Moses' walk with God appears to become real at the burning bush. Perhaps he had something of a relationship with Him before, but that encounter in the wilderness jumpstarted his destiny. It deposited within him a very strong spiritual seed, one that was not easy for him to accept. In fact, he did everything he could think of, even beg, to get out of the demand of Heaven God had placed on him.

He had no desire to try his faith. God did several amazing miracles in front of him to prove that he could trust Him, but Moses still said, "I can't do this! I'm not a good speaker at all. No one will accept me."

We can feel the weight in God's response: "Who made your mouth?" He replied. "Who made you the way you are? Was it not I? Now go, and I will give you everything you need."

But that was not enough. "Oh, God — just send somebody else." Moses flat out refused. He saw miracles and signs; he stood barefoot on holy ground and faced the burning bush, but he still told God, "I'm not Your man."

This frightened refusal takes place at the beginning of one of the most elaborate, most amazing stories in the Bible. If you'll excuse my name calling, this coward is the man who was later used to dismantle the most powerful empire on the Earth; he parted the Red Sea, talked to God face to face, made water flow out of a rock, wrote the first five books of the Bible, and went down in history as one of the greatest heroes of the faith. He changed the world, but he started at the burning bush, where he grumbled and complained and said he couldn't do it. God had to mold him into the great man of faith he became.

MOSES AND WAITING FOR HOPE

After this radical impartation of faith, Moses moved into the hope stage.

Hope can be simply defined as believing that God is a good God, and that no matter what happens, God is still a good God. This is what heroes are made of — people who are willing to believe in God's good nature, even if it seems that things are going badly and evil is thriving. Moses started with faith, but I think it wasn't until God unleashed the plagues on Egypt that he slowly began to understand that God is truly good.

When he threw his staff down before Pharaoh, it turned into a snake. That (surprisingly) wasn't the miracle, because Pharaoh's magicians were able to turn their staffs into snakes as well. The miracle was that Moses' snake consumed the magicians' snakes, proving that his God was stronger. Instantly, I imagine that his faith jumped. *God can do what He said He was going to do! He meant it!*

But what happened as a result of that faith builder? Pharaoh doubled the burden on the people. Instead of being delivered, they suddenly had to meet impossible demands, and it seemed like a bad deal for them.

In the face of apparent failure, no doubt Moses was forced

to rethink everything he had assumed would work out. *Is this really going to end well?* Not only did he have his own doubts to deal with, but he also had to struggle beneath the doubts of more than two million people. They began to grumble against him.

This sort of situation is why hope is vital. It goes hand in hand with faith, for if we don't have hope — a firm belief that God is good and the situation *will* turn out well — we won't make it through the hard, difficult times when our faith is tested. Without hope, we will give up and think, *God must not be truly good. He didn't do what I needed Him to do.* Without a foundation of hope, we won't wait to see if the situation is going to work out after all.

One of the great truths of God is that it will *always* work out. It may not work out the way we were expecting or wanting; we may not fully understand His plan until after death, but God's promises to us *always* work out. They are always "Yes" and "Amen" (2 Corinthians 1:20). Hope is what enables us to cling to His Word and continue to trust Him, even when all we see is darkness.

The hope of intercessors is what gets tried. As seers, we know what God has given us. We have seen it or sensed it; we know that He wants to do something and that He's working to see it done, but sometimes we lose hope that what we've been praying for will actually come about. All of these questions are issues of hope: *Will my country come to repentance? Will my children be in sync with God? Will they stop fighting Him? Did God know what He was doing when He selected these leaders? Did God know what He was doing when He gave me this job? This spouse? These children?*

Of course, God knew what He was doing. If we don't have hope, questions like these may cause us to forget who He is. Over time, they will wear us down, and eventually, we won't have the strength to wait on the Lord, as the Bible tells us to do over and over again: "Wait on the Lord; be of good courage, and He shall strengthen your heart" (Psalm 27:14, NKJV). This is a promise. Wait, and He will strengthen you. Again, hope is what enables us to wait, to hold on to a vision, and to be patient as God's plans come to fruition.

Being an intercessor is a very serious thing. Not all seers have taken on the intercessory role, but many of us have. Our hope is the bridge between the promises of God and the people to whom He made them. If the bridge is weak, or just doesn't exist, the people may not make it to the other side, and the promises of God in their lives may not be completely realized. If we give in to doubt, fear, or pessimism concerning the people God has laid on our hearts, it is similar to letting go of their destinies.

> "AGAIN, HOPE IS WHAT ENABLES US TO WAIT, TO HOLD ON TO A VISION, AND TO BE PATIENT AS GOD'S PLANS COME TO FRUITION."

Please understand me here. By writing this, I am not encouraging you to "try harder." I would not do that. Instead, I want to strengthen your hope. God knows that the way is steep, the burden is heavy, and that it is difficult to get to the top. He is an intercessor Himself (Hebrews 7:25); He knows what this journey is like. He is more than familiar with this hill, and He knows what will help us make it those last few feet to the top.

LOVE: THE DIFFERENCE BETWEEN MOSES AND BALAAM

The Apostle Paul wrote that our hope will not disappoint us (Romans 5:5). As leaders walk into what seers have seen and intercessors have prayed for, a *huge* window of opportunity opens for the people to enter in as well; that is the labor of love. As intercessors, if we don't love the people we're praying for, we won't be able to make it those final, last steps up the mountain. Our faith may be strong; our hope may bridge the gap, but without the commitment of love, the burden will not reach the summit.

Love was Moses' trying point. He believed in *faith* that God wanted the people freed from slavery. He had *hope* that it would come to pass, that he would be able to see it with his own eyes, but all of this took place in a relatively short amount of time. The window for the people took much longer — forty years longer — to be realized, and this was where the test of love came in. As an intercessor, Moses held the destiny of the entire nation of Israel in his hands. Literally. When the people sinned with the golden calf and deserved death, God allowed Moses to decide what would happen with them.

"Let Me wipe them out," God said, "and I'll start a whole new people just with you."

Would that have fulfilled the faith? Absolutely. God wanted to have a people all His own, and having Moses' descendents alone would have fulfilled that.

Would that have fulfilled the hope? Yes. His will would have happened on Earth, just as God said it would, not to mention that the situation would have been extremely good for Moses.

But would it have fulfilled the love? No, because the people wouldn't have entered in.

If Moses hadn't loved Israel right then, in that moment, they would not have survived. Their destiny was in his hands, but because he loved them, he wanted them to live.

Again, if he hadn't had faith, the deliverance wouldn't have begun. If he hadn't had hope, it would not have continued. But if he hadn't had love, no one would have gotten to participate, and the history of Israel, and the world, would look very different today.

Moses and Balaam, whom we discussed in the last chapter, were contemporaries who shared several characteristics. Balaam also had great faith: He knew what God had said. He also had great hope: He knew that God would show His nature, which is why he didn't dare curse the people himself. He had a gifting; he had the demand of Heaven on him. But he did not love the people, and so, instead of sparing them, he found a loophole, worked it to his advantage, and the people were cursed. Scripture says that he "formulated a plan" on how to destroy them. Because of their sin, the people stopped being able to enter in, which created a negative pressure in the spiritual realm and dumped curses, not blessings, into their laps. Instead of loving them, Balaam added toward their destruction.

> THE WINDOW FOR THE PEOPLE IS FIRST OPENED BY FAITH AND HOPE, AND THEN IT IS KEPT OPEN BY LOVE.

The window for the people is first opened by faith and hope, and then it is kept open by love. Moses kept this window open. It took forty years for the people to enter in, but he stubbornly kept the window open, wanting them to possess what God had promised them. In the end, they did, and he was the one who was not able to enter. If Moses had not loved them and stood in the gap for them that day, he would not have later struck the rock in anger and been denied entrance into the Promised Land. If he had not asked God to stay His hand, he would have received what he had been hoping, praying, and having faith for all those years. He would have touched it with his own hands, instead of having to look at it only from a distance.

But his love was for the people, and so he unwittingly gave up what he could have had, so they could have it. That is a love commitment — a strong, tangible covenant of love. It can pain the one who bears it. It's heavy, and the way is steep, and the hill is slanted. But the journey is worth the reward (Hebrews 12:2).

I am convinced that intercession was birthed in Egypt, because that was where God's people first learned to cry out. God sent Moses to deliver them because of one stated reason: "I'm doing this," He said, "because I've heard the cries of My people." Their prayers moved Him. He heard them; He saw their burdens, and then He acted on their behalf.

God touched my heart. I was preparing to teach on intercession, and He told me, "You can't tell them what to do without refreshing them. It's such a heavy burden, and I see it."

He wants us to be refreshed. He is not blind to the weights we carry. He knows what we're struggling to haul up the mountain, and His heart is for us to be revived. He wants to come alongside us and bear our burdens with us, so that we begin to realize that we are not alone — something that many of us have a hard time believing. Lugging the rocks up the hill is difficult enough, but if we believe that we are the only one doing so, we're shouldering an unnecessary burden that will end up isolating us.

Every good parent wants his or her children to know, "You belong with me. You are like me, and you carry my attributes." There are many intercessors and seers who don't feel that they are truly part of their church family because they don't see how they are like their brothers and sisters. But God wants us to know that we're not outside this family. Every single foolish, silly, mistaken, misplaced thing we've ever done *will* bear fruit as God comes along, takes the wasted years, and says, "I'm going to give you favor here. You will have blessing in this."

When refreshing comes to us, we realize there is more — a lot more, which we couldn't have faith for earlier because the burden was consuming too much of us. As our hope returns to us, we realize there is more to see, more to interact with, more to touch, and — most importantly — there is a greater understanding of God's heart that has been waiting for us this entire time. Whenever God refreshes us, we come to realize once again how perfect He is, how strong He is, and how much we don't have to be. This day, be at peace.

PROPHETIC & SEER Q&A:

QUESTION: When God speaks, is it a spine-chilling, "life changing" event? Are there different levels of hearing? Is hearing and seeing a daily thing or only for the few great saints of the past?

ANSWER: I believe that God speaks to everyone and that He is communicating constantly. Every time He speaks, the universe changes. It *is* a spine-chilling, "life changing" event, though it may not always appear that way to us on the receiving end. Often He whispers so quietly that it is very easy for us to miss it. He does this because He wants us to "tune" ourselves to Him.

Elijah saw an incredible display of power. The fire of God consumed water and rock and proved that God was God and not Baal. But after that experience, Elijah became frightened and ran for his life from Jezebel. In that moment, he didn't need another thunderous act; he needed the still, quiet whisper of God in the cave (1 Kings 19:12).

The whisper is what establishes relationship. God will often speak to us in a way that we could dismiss if we wanted to, because He wants us to act in faith, to believe it is Him. He does this to build intimacy and relationship with us.

There are times when His voice is unbelievably spine chilling and changes everything. But that may not happen very often, and it may not happen for everybody. Just as it is in everyday personal interactions, loud communications are usually not meant for moments of intimacy. Huge presentations and banners in the sky aren't private messages of love; they are for the crowd. When God speaks to us in a loud way that leaves no room for doubt, it's usually so that He can change the world through us in that moment.

For intimacy and relationship, we need the still, quiet voice. If we don't miss it when He whispers, then we really won't miss it when He speaks to us loudly, in a way that rattles the Earth.

CHAPTER 12

HOW DO WE GET BETTER AT THIS?
WAYS TO INCREASE OUR FAITH

In the first chapter, I said that my primary goal in writing this book is to help you grow closer to Jesus. Relationship with Him is the foundation of our faith, and as you've read this book, hopefully you have realized that the principal purpose of the seer gifting is for us to fall deeper in love with God.

For a season in my life, I would ask God on a daily basis, "What do You want to say to me?"

He would reply, "Jim, I love you."

This went on for an entire year, and I finally told Him, "That's all You tell me. All day long. Every time I ask, You say the same thing. Why do You not tell me anything else?"

"Because you need to hear that," He replied.

It was simple and unassuming, and it changed my life. I came out of that season with a much deeper understanding of how

God feels about me.

We are on this journey to have our lives changed — to know Him better and to learn how to communicate with His heart. As we train in our giftings, we mature in Him (Hebrews 5:14); we grow in our knowledge of Him and His ways. We become more and more amazed at who He is, how intimate He desires to be with us, and how often He wants to speak with us.

Many churches and individuals struggle with their intimacy with God not because their faith is weak or nonexistent but because they aren't willing to make mistakes. They feel a desperate need to be the special one who does everything right the first time. The result is that when God invites them to participate in signs, wonders, and greater intimacy with Him, they have difficulty doing so because they feel the need to be perfect in it.

But God is more interested in *us* than our success. As seers, this is very important to understand, because it will naturally and dramatically cause our faith and trust in Him to increase. We don't have to focus on "getting it right" or pulling off a perfect performance as we learn to use our giftings. Instead, if we have committed our ways to Him and have chosen to walk with Him humbly, He will turn our disheveled attempts into great victories. We can do our best and then commit the rest to Him. That is enough.

In Philippians 2, Paul exhorted us to work out our salvation with "fear and trembling." This is very different than being afraid of failure. Obviously, Paul isn't suggesting we be anxious or timid. Instead, he's urging us to cling to God, the One who is our hope — to realize that He is the perfection of who we are and what we do. By ourselves, we cannot accomplish anything of true value. He is the only One who can do that.

As we seek to increase our faith and utilize our seer giftings in truth and godliness, we will naturally find ourselves clinging to God more and more, because we will realize how small we are and how big He is. Sometimes we will make mistakes, and sometimes we may fail. There will be times when we interpret metaphors poorly and times when we think God meant one thing and He really meant something else. These things don't happen to us because we're not as worthy as another person or not mature enough; they happen because we're human and we are growing. Again, the only way we will be able to do anything of worth is if He makes it happen through His grace (2 Corinthians 12:9). This should alleviate any pressure we feel to perform.

Doing something poorly isn't necessarily a sign of our immaturity. If our best shot is a "bad" shot, God can come and fill in the cracks and cause our efforts to be more than enough. If we are willing to do things even if it means doing them at a level that seems inadequate, God can use us to do things well, because then we will know that He is the force

> WE ARE ON THIS JOURNEY TO HAVE OUR LIVES CHANGED — TO KNOW HIM BETTER AND TO LEARN HOW TO COMMUNICATE WITH HIS HEART.

behind our actions and not we ourselves. Humility allows our imperfect actions to be perfect witnesses and signs of God's goodness.

When I say this, however, I don't mean to imply that trusting God to use our mistakes somehow nullifies the need to be humble and correctable. On the contrary, we should expect God to use others to point out our mistakes so we can respond to Him by responding to their correction. We have a responsibility of knowing when to be quiet and pray and when to act. We shouldn't ignore our discernment, rush to do whatever we think we should do, and then trust God to fix it. What I am saying is that we should do what we feel God is leading us to do when He leads us to do it and be open to being wrong, knowing that God can use the mistakes that we don't cover up or deny. Then, as other people see that we are willing to be used in spite of our faults, their hearts will be further opened to the kindness and love of God.

HOW DO WE GROW IN OUR GIFTINGS?

We don't need to know everything there is to know about our seer giftings, our destinies, or where we're going next in life; we just need to press forward in knowing God, because, with time, that will answer every other question. Matthew 6:33 communicated this quite clearly: "'But seek first His kingdom and His righteousness, and all these things will be added to you.'"

This simple, humble path is the one He has set before us, and it is applicable to matters of faith. Jesus went on to say in Matthew 13:12, "'For whoever has, to him more shall be given, and he will have an abundance; but whoever does not have, even what he has shall be taken away from him.'" Our belief in God grows the more we believe Him. Our faith in Him grows the more we walk in it. Faith is like muscle mass; if we don't use it, it atrophies, but if we exercise it, it becomes stronger.

Stepping out in faith and thereby growing in faith often

requires us to take risks. Each of us has a "growth zone" — an area that is outside our comfort zones but inside what we have faith for. This is where growth takes place. Taking risks tends to be uncomfortable, but it isn't necessarily complicated. It can mean bringing the picture or impression back to God and asking Him about it when we previously would have just dismissed it. It can mean interpreting a dream we didn't think we'd be able to interpret or being willing to tell other people what we're seeing in the spiritual realm. For the more analytical-minded among us, it can mean asking God to give us revelation and then simply believing that He is. We asked Him to speak to us. Why would we doubt His desire or ability to do so?

One of our Stir the Water users recently wrote in and asked how she can know that she isn't simply making things up as she does the seer exercises on the site. She is very analytical, so she is concerned that all she is doing is strengthening her imagination.

God has not given us a spirit of fear (2 Timothy 1:7), so any fear we have that suggests what we're seeing or experiencing is "just us" isn't God telling us to be cautious — it is us being fearful. It could also be the enemy trying to influence us. He doesn't want us to do anything that would further our relationship with God.

We should be more concerned with being ruled by fear than we are with being ruled by our imaginations. If, as analytical people, we're being ruled by our imaginations, we'll figure that out. But if we are ruled by fear, we won't be able to see or think clearly, and until we break out of that cycle, growth could be difficult. We should be much more concerned with being ruled by fear than with somehow being fooled.

So if we want to have greater faith, we need to start with the faith we have today, even if the only steps we can take today are baby steps. We can do this by setting very doable goals for ourselves, such as seeing one thing a day, and then not feeling like we failed if we aren't successful. We should just do the best we can.

The key to growth in faith is putting ourselves into situations where we have to trust God. We may feel like we're falling short or not doing enough, but if we give it time, we'll be able to look back and see how much we have grown.

ENCOURAGE ONE ANOTHER AND GET FEEDBACK

In order to grow in our faith, we first need to use the faith we have. Second, we should seek out like-minded people whose faith will provoke our own, and vice versa. We can practice giftings together, compare metaphorical interpretations, talk about what we have experienced, ask questions, and seek confirmation and feedback.

Encouraging feedback can be very important. I remember the first time I stood up in front of my church and gave words to members of the congregation. By the time I had finished, I was convinced that nothing I'd said was accurate. The congregation had sat there and stared at me with blank looks. One man had been shaking his head.

After the service, my pastor went up to every person I'd ministered to and asked if the word was correct. This upset my wife, but I found it reassuring because I wasn't going to do that. It would be like telling someone, "Jesus loves you," then saying later, "I'm actually not sure that was true. What do you think?"

When we speak into others' lives, we use the faith we have, and once we use it, it's gone. This is why some of us begin to doubt ourselves after giving a word. *Why did I think that was accurate? How do I know for sure?* Depending on the situation, it can be very beneficial for someone else to find out if the other person or people thought our words were accurate. Encouraging feedback will grow our faith because we will re-

> IN ORDER TO GROW IN OUR FAITH, WE FIRST NEED TO USE THE FAITH WE HAVE.

alize how much God actually does speak to us and through us. Next time, we will be able to speak into others' lives with more confidence, and it won't be so hard for us to take a greater risk.

My pastor hadn't given the word, so he was able to follow up with the people. He then came back to me and said, "Jim, did you know those words were right?"

My wife replied, "Of course, they're right!"

But I said, "Really? Then maybe the ones I've given before are right, too!" My faith grew because of that accountability and encouragement.

SEEK ENCOURAGEMENT FROM GOD

Third, after we have acted in faith, we should not only welcome feedback from other people, but we should also develop the habit of seeking confirmation and encouragement from God. How does *He* think we did? Does *He* like what we said and how we said it? What could we have done better? His answers to these questions will greatly grow our faith, as well as our understanding of His heart. His opinion of us is more important, and more realistic, than any opinion we could have of ourselves.

At different times in my life, I spoke to groups of people and afterward felt like I had done a good job. My presentation was prepared, clear, and smoothly delivered, but when I asked God how I had done, He surprised me.

You didn't talk about what I wanted you to talk about.

Then there were other times when I *knew* I had done a horrible job. I was talking about an unfamiliar topic, wasn't prepared for it, and stumbled through the delivery. But when I asked God how I had done, He replied, *That was great!*

"How was that great?"

You spoke about what I wanted you to speak about. You did a great job.

When we are willing to do something poorly (that is, when we are willing to show our lack of skill), He can use us to do something great. From an earthly perspective, what we have done may not look like anything of worth, but it is to Him, and that is what matters. We need to calibrate our minds, wills, and emotions to His mind, His will, and His emotions. Even when we completely fail in something, didn't do a good job, or should have done it a different way, His loving feedback will give us enormous encouragement and draw us closer to Him — and it will also be a benefit to others, because when we are in communion with His heart, the people God has called us to influence will be able to tell.

IN CONCLUSION

The three main ways we can grow our faith are by using it, seeking encouragement and feedback from others, and seeking encouragement from God. As we make these a part of our lives, we will see growth in tangible ways.

There is no set method or concrete list of steps to experience more of God in our lives. The key is simply to be with Him. So on a daily basis, be creative. Ask Him random questions in random places such as the subway, the commute to work, or the office. Get in the habit of looking for Him near you. See what He is doing. Practice looking into the spiritual realm wherever you go, whatever you're doing. Sometimes I will ask God, "What are You wanting to show me in this moment?" Or, "If You could tell me only one thing today, what would it be?" This second question is particularly helpful if you tend to be overwhelmed by all the things you're seeing or if you have trouble seeing anything at all. Don't feel as if you need to ask Him every question you can think of or do every seer exercise you've ever heard of. Just be with Him and see what happens.

One of the most popular Prophetic & Seer Exercises on Stir the Water is called "Seeing Jesus." Its purpose is to train people to see Him everywhere. To look for Him. It helps us realize His proximity, His ways, His heart, and how He is with us literally all the time. We will be going through this exercise in the next chapter.

But before we get to it, I want to bless you in your gifting. Many of you have a deep understanding of God that He has built up within you through times of trial and error, of triumph and sorrow, of seeing His faithfulness, and of experiencing His presence and friendship. I want to affirm that within you. What God has taught you in the quiet is not minimal, unimportant, or less profound than the experiences of others that may seem grander or more public. The way that God communicates to *you*, personally, is valuable and weighty. I bless that within you and pray that your eyes will be further opened to Him as He moves and acts and reveals Himself to you.

CHAPTER 13

"SEEING JESUS"

A STIR THE WATER PROPHETIC & SEER EXERCISE

In this chapter, we will be doing a simple, practical exercise that will noticeably affect how you communicate with Jesus. It will also probably affect how *often* you communicate with Jesus! No matter how experienced you are as a seer, this exercise will position you so that your faith will grow.

Before we begin, there are three elements that we need to discuss. First, relax. You will be able to do this much better if you aren't worried about doing it well.

Second, don't dismiss what comes to you, even if it seems like it was just your imagination. Instead, follow it through and see what happens. It is common for people to receive something in a step that they feel isn't what God is trying to show them; perhaps it doesn't seem to fit other things they have seen or it doesn't immediately make sense.

Third, nurture an atmosphere of faith and expectancy. If you have ignored something in the past and assumed it couldn't possibly be God, pay attention to it now. *Expect* to hear from Him. Sometimes a small nudge of faith is the only thing that keeps us from dismissing something that could change our lives.

Jesus said that He did only what He saw His Father doing (John 5:19). He was doing the essence of the exercise you are about to do. He looked to see where the Father was and what He was doing through the presence of the Holy Spirit, and then He mirrored His own life after those things. None of what you see during this exercise could possibly be any stranger than what Jesus must have seen: He put mud on a blind man's eyes! He must have seen the Father doing that.

Do each of the following seven steps in order. Don't skip any of them. Write down what you sense, even if you think it was just your imagination. Afterward, when you read over what you've written, you will most likely be able to sense what was "just you" and what God was whispering to your spirit.

"SEEING JESUS" EXERCISE
STEP 1

Ask the Lord to show you where Jesus is in the room. Write down and describe what you sense.

By writing it down, you allow the revelation to move from what you think *might* have been revealed to you to something that God actually revealed to you. It escalates the revelation and strengthens your spiritual senses.

Also, write down how it came to you. You may actually see it with your physical eyes, or it could be just a notion or impression; it may seem like you're making it up. In fact, if you feel like you're not getting anything, *guess* where Jesus is. If you were to imagine Him in the room, where would He be? God created your imagination, and He will use it to speak to you.

Often, revelation first comes as a vague feeling that will resolve to more specific details as you pay attention to it and bring your other spiritual senses to bear. This first step of the exercise can start like that. You sort of sense He is there and that He could be in a specific spot, and then you may start to get pictorial-type impressions.

STEP 2

Describe what the Lord is doing. If you already did this in Step 1, go into greater detail here. You may want to take a second look.

Often when I'm doing this exercise with a group, people will ask me to explain this step. When we notice Jesus is with us, we don't always remember to pay attention to what He is doing. Why is He next to us and not standing across the room? Is He carrying something? What is it? Is He looking at something? What is He doing?

We see what we look for, and so we need to pay attention to what God is doing. It is possible to miss the depth of this experience simply because we didn't take the time to stop and look.

STEP 3

Describe what Jesus is wearing. If you didn't see this detail before, look for it now.

Keep in mind that this could be metaphorical as well. For instance, if you saw Jesus dressed as a farmer, what would you expect Him to be doing? You'd expect Him to be farming. If you saw Him dressed as a plumber, there may be something clogging your system that He has come to wash out of you.

STEP 4

Ask Jesus why He is here. Describe what you hear.

STEP 5

Ask Jesus how you can cooperate with what He is doing.

This step requires vulnerability, because it can be self-disclosing. There have been times when I have been doing this exercise publicly, and at this step, God rebukes me over my attitudes, doctrines, or sin. My heart is exposed in front of everyone.

There is a level of safety in doing these exercises by yourself, but you will grow more if you do them with others.

STEP 6

Ask Jesus how He feels about the person He is standing near.

This could be you, or if you're doing this exercise in a group, it could be someone else. He may be standing near one person but looking at another person across the room.

Keep in mind that what you see now may or may not seem to fit into what you saw before. This does not mean it is wrong or that you are making it up.

STEP 7

Ask Jesus how you can have His heart for the person He just showed you.

Again, this may be you. Write down His response, no matter how odd it sounds and even if you have no plans to share your answers with anyone.

EXERCISE FOLLOW-UP

Put away what you've written for a while — maybe a day or even a few days.

When you come back to it, you will be amazed at how the words seem to leap off the page. In most cases, you will be able to sense in your spirit what was Him and what may have been simply your own thoughts. If you experience confusion, do the exercise again.

There is great value in repeated practice. If you do a specific seer exercise one to five times, you will have an introductory understanding of how your gifting is used in the area addressed. When you have done it twenty-one times or more, you are forming a habit of using your gifting in the area the exercise targets.

In conclusion, Jesus builds intimacy with us during our periods of low anointing. The "Seeing Jesus" exercise, as well as the other exercises on Stir the Water, are very good for those times, when we feel like we aren't seeing, hearing, or experiencing anything. If we listen to God only during the times of high anointing, the high times get even higher, but the low times get lower. However, if we listen to God during the low anointed times, the low times get higher, and the high times get even higher. In other words, we mature.

Even if you are doing this exercise quietly by yourself, it is best to do it the first time in a gathering of Christians. Jesus said in Matthew 18:20, "'For where two or three have gathered together in My name, I am there in their midst.'" In this setting, it is biblical to expect Jesus to be there and just a practical step of faith to look for Him.

ABOUT THE AUTHOR

Jim Driscoll is the director and founder of www.stirthewater.com, an online interactive ministry designed to help people grow in their prophetic and seer giftings. He operates in a strong prophetic and seer anointing and has a developed gift for interpreting dreams. Traveling throughout the United States and Europe, he teaches on dreams and visions and leads dream interpretation classes. He and his wife, Mims, and their six children live in South Carolina.

Bibliography and Suggested Resources

Virkler, Mark. *Dialogue with God*. Alachua, FL: Bridge-Logos, 1986.

Brother Lawrence. *The Practice of the Presence of God*.

Driscoll, Jim, and Mapes, Zach. *The Seer Course*. For more information, visit www.stirthewater.com.

Peretti, Frank E. *This Present Darkness*. Wheaton, IL: Crossway Books, original printing 1986.

Peretti, Frank E. *Piercing the Darkness*. Wheaton, IL: Crossway Books, original printing 1989.

Conner, Kevin J. *Interpreting the Symbols & Types*. Portland, OR: City Christian Publishing, 1988.

Milligan, Ira. *Understanding the Dreams You Dream*. Shippensburg, PA: Treasure House, 1997.

Ryken, Leland; Wilhoit, James C.; Longman III, Tremper. *Dictionary of Biblical Imagery*. Westmont, IL: InterVarsity Press, 1998.

www.scripture4all.org
www.ancient-hebrew.org
www.stirthewater.com
www.stirthewater.com/dreams

APPENDIX 1
STIR THE WATER

www.stirthewater.com

Stir the Water is an online interactive ministry designed to help people grow in their prophetic and seer giftings. It does this mainly through prophetic and seer exercises that implement Hebrews 5:14 (NKJV): "Solid food belongs to those who are of full age, that is, those who by reason of use have their senses exercised to discern both good and evil." You will grow in your spiritual senses as you use them, and as you use them, you will increase in spiritual maturity.

As you practice your giftings by doing the exercises on this site, you will experience growth in spiritual matters as well as in your giftings themselves.

Please visit www.stirthewater.com/free for more information and a free trial offer.

Appendix 2
Interpret My Dream

Interpret My Dream
Interpreter Training Website
™

www.stirthewater.com/dreams

Interpret My Dream, part of the Stir the Water Network, empowers people to become effective translators of God's metaphorical dream language. Imagine that He has written you hundreds of letters about how He loves you, His plans for you, and issues for you to pray about, but each letter is written in a mysterious metaphorical language. Wouldn't you want to learn that language?

Interpret My Dream was created to help train the Church to understand this wonderful and mystifying form of communication from God. The online tools help you learn biblically based interpretive processes and practice that understanding at your own pace.

Please visit www.stirthewater.com/free for more information and a free trial offer.

Appendix 3

My grandmother was there to witness her own funeral, which is in line with the biblical function of believers who are with God (John 11:25).

Necromancy is the process of communicating with the dead using soulish or demonic means. The Bible clearly spells out that the practice is evil. However, the Bible also allows that there might be times when God orchestrates a meeting between a living person and a person who is with Him, and in that case, it is not necromancy but a God-ordained experience:

1. Jesus, Peter, James, and John interacted with Moses (Matthew 17), who the Bible clearly says was dead (Joshua 1:2). Jesus said in John 14:12 that we would do all He did and more.

2. The Bible talks about the great cloud of witnesses: people of faith who surround us and observe our activities on Earth (Hebrews 12:1–2). As they are witnesses, it is possible that God may send them to "witness" to us about something of God.

3. In Jesus' parable of Lazarus and the rich man, He said that Lazarus wouldn't be sent back to witness to the rich man's family because they wouldn't change; Jesus did not say that he couldn't be sent or that he wouldn't be sent if the family would respond (Luke 16).

4. Jesus implied that the spirit of Lazarus (Mary and Martha's brother) was still present and hanging around while his body was "asleep" (John 11).

BEING A Seer

LEARN WHO YOU ARE AS A SEER, THE DYNAMICS BETWEEN THE SPIRITUAL AND NATURAL REALMS, AND YOUR ROLE IN BOTH.

2 DISK SET BY JIM DRISCOLL

Learn how ancient Hebrew defines *seer*.

Understand the pictures and visions you see so that you can know what to do about them.

Be proactive in your gifting - help yourself and others understand the gap between the natural and the supernatural.

Learn about spiritual pressure - how it affects you and where it comes from.

Participate in an exercise that will open your spiritual eyes to see Jesus in the room.

Order online at:
www.stirthewater.com/store

REVELATION THROUGH
Intimacy
BECOMING A FRIEND OF GOD

A lot of people feel like they can't interact with God. They don't feel close to Him, and they don't know how to begin to communicate with Him on a daily basis.

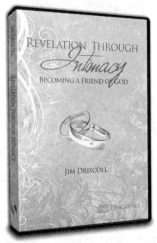

2 Disk Set by Jim Driscoll

Jump-start the process of learning to receive and understand revelation.

Order online at:
www.stirthewater.com/store